BREAKING TI

Breaking the Mould

EDITED BY GERALD COATES

KINGSWAY PUBLICATIONS
EASTBOURNE

ISBN 0 86065 699 3

Printed in Great Britain for
KINGSWAY PUBLICATIONS LTD
Lottbridge Drove, Eastbourne, E Sussex BN23 6NT by
Clays Ltd, St. Ives plc
Typeset by J&L Composition Ltd, Filey, North Yorkshire

Contents

I

The Shape of the Prophetic Church to Come

Gerald Coates

Gerald Coates is Director of the Pioneer Trust and leader of the Pioneer Team. Their main role is to care for churches in a partnership relationship, plant churches, and train leaders and evangelists through their TIE (Training In Evangelism) Teams. He is known as a speaker both nationally and internationally, and has written six books, including his autobiography An Intelligent Fire *and* Kingdom Now! *a more detailed manifesto than is contained in his two chapters in this book.*

The church must change its shape or die. Major sections are dying both spiritually and numerically. People are losing hope. No hope—no faith. Or perhaps I should say, no faith therefore no hope.

Let us consider historic denominations first. Institutional Christianity lost one million members in the 1970s and another half million in the 1980s. In that time the Church of England closed over 1,000 churches, and the Methodist Church lost over one-third of its members.

Many bishops and clergy are known for denying Christ's virgin birth and bodily resurrection. At least one has gone on record as saying that the God of the Bible is 'cultic' if not 'the devil himself'! Sadly this actually gives some leaders further acceptance and seems to aid promotion in the Synod and even in Free Church hierarchies. Should you happen to agree with almost any of Mr

Major's policies, however, you are looked upon as being positively suspect, unspiritual and almost a heretic! There is a massive anti-government left-wing power block in the Synod. And this from those who own millions of pounds in property—not just church property, but housing estates, offices, land and treasure. Agree with the authority of God and with Scripture and you are booed. Disagree with the authority of the government and you are applauded.

There are many in the Church of England who are seeking to be true to Christ, to Scripture and to the call of God on their lives. They work hard at serving the community around them. (There are still many such leaders within the Anglican communion despite the press giving column inches to leaders whose theology is as organised as a sack of spanners.) But evangelicals have been largely regarded as being from another planet and belonging to another age. Evangelical bishops have always been given a hard time in the Church of England and our present evangelical archbishop will be given an even harder time.

Keen to woo the hierarchy, NEAC '88 (National Evangelical Anglican Celebration) gave Dr Runcie a remarkable ovation after his address before over 3,000 evangelical leaders. One evangelical, Spirit-filled Anglican leader visiting our church from Singapore told me, 'Many of Dr Runcie's bishops don't believe in the resurrection.' He laughed: 'Even outright pagans in Singapore believe that Jesus rose from the dead and is alive today!'

But it would be unfair and unjust to spotlight the Anglicans alone. Many within the other denominational hierarchies are in the same position (with some wonderful and notable exceptions). So you can be a practising homosexual, pay scant regard to Scripture, ridicule the traditional body of belief (doctrine) and you'll be at worst tolerated if not positively applauded. This deception has not come overnight, it has been nurtured over a long period of time. It was given room by leaders who were unable or unwilling to bring discipline to the immoral or heretical.

Creating a different sort of church

However, this publication is not about the declining church, the unbelieving church or the church of the past. It is not about righting the wrongs of the institutional church, though I admire and respect those who are working to bring renewal and restoration to denominational Christianity. We at Pioneer do not feel we are called to invest the rest of our lives in that direction. I'm not sure we have sufficient time or resources to invest anyway. We must create a completely different sort of church in Britain. And Pioneer is not alone in that assessment. Many other 'New Church' streams, teams and networks are doing the same. It is slow; we are making mistakes. But we are also seeking to work hand in hand with all those who love the Lord Jesus, are unashamed evangelicals in faith and practice, and want to see revival in our land.

As is often God's way, he takes the powerless and those marginalised to do exploits for him. After twenty years of marginalisation charismatic evangelicals have the reins in many areas of church life. The largest Christian conference is charismatic—Spring Harvest, attracting 80,000. Most evangelistic and church-planting teams are evangelical charismatics. The plethora of books and tapes being churned out are largely charismatic, emphasising kingdom theology and godly living. The March for Jesus across Europe and, latterly, America was initiated by charismatics from the 'New Churches'. The resources of these churches, plus charismatic Christians within denominational churches, who are seeking to be relevant and radical, are being drawn together from various levels in a wide range of networking activities. But there are dangers. History is littered with examples of God 'giving grace to the humble' and God exalting the humble which is invariably followed by 'how are the mighty fallen'. So this new wine needs new wineskins; the old are inflexible and likely to burst, losing both the wine and doing irreparable damage to the skin. I believe the majority of New Churches are still flexible enough to contain that wine.

So what should the shape of the church be like? How can

we shape it from within? How do we stop past and present structures of exciting flexibility becoming inflexible and resistant to change?

This introductory chapter will be deliberately broad in its base, envisioning in its motivation and at times radical in its approach. We are not radical enough. The rest of the chapters will deal with specific issues and subjects.

Not radical enough?

There are two important words both pronounced the same. One is the word 'radical' which means 'to go to the root of things'. Then there is 'radicle', which is a part of the seed which becomes the root. Western traditional Christianity has chopped itself off from its historic, biblical roots. That is why it is dying. You can't chop yourself off from your roots and expect to blossom and flourish. It is often claimed that the New Churches have chopped themselves off from their roots, but in fact it is the New Churches who are seeking to be *true* to their biblical authentic roots. Major sections of our historic churches have scorned and removed the principles many were once burned at the stake for. That is why historic Christianity is losing its distinctive voice. That's why we have moved from balanced belief to caustic compromise and eventually to a sellout. In an attempt to build bridges and create understanding, many have changed sides altogether and will be found on the wrong side of God.

Only a radical approach will enable Jesus to rebuild his church and see multitudes added who are, it seems, without hope and without God. To be radical and reshape the church we must go to the root of things.

Radical and prophetic

The godly radical of today will be seen as prophetic tomorrow. But not everything that is controversial is prophetic. Not everything that fails to fit in with the current system of things is of God's

Spirit. To be prophetic is to carry God's heart and God's word which always goes to the real root. God never deals with cosmetics.

Prophets are given visions, and therefore goals. As Peter Wagner has said, 'Power is released through setting positive goals that otherwise remain dormant.' Prophets who carry God's heart either see those goals or what has to be done to remove the obstacles that hinder us attaining them. For to be prophetic entails seeing and preparing for the future. Prophecy is not usually predictive. In fact there are only two predictive prophecies in the whole of the Acts of the Apostles, a record that covers a period of at least thirty years.

It has to be said that some so-called prophets have been driven by pride, ignorance, mega-sincerity or soulish excitement. They have created concerns and even chaos as they speak 'in the name of the Lord'. But one thing is clear. We cannot fulfil our task without being prophetic. The only thing false prophecy does is to show us the need of *true* prophets. The faked and the forged obviously indicate that there must be an original and the authentic. But when we say prophetic, we are not talking about well-informed hunches. We need divine revelation. It is a light so bright that it makes all other light dark. It is saying goodbye to yesterday's problems (and blessings) because we've seen a new tomorrow. The kingdom of God therefore does not consist of dragging the past into the present, but dragging the future into the present.

Jesus and the church

Jesus Christ is our Prophet, Priest and King. The church also has a prophetic, priestly and kingly ministry. Being *prophetic* means bringing God's word. As A W Tozer commented, 'Truth is true at all times so the teacher teaches truth at all times. But the prophet must bring particular truth to a particular people in a particular situation.' The *priest* is a reconciler. He brings people together with God and reconciles people to one another. In the church it is normally the pastors and the shepherds who do that, but in a sense even the evangelist has a priestly ministry in seeing men and women reconciled to God. Our *kingly* role has little to do with human relationships. We're never asked to take authority (the authority of a king) over our friends or folk in the church. We're told to take authority over the enemy. We have plenty of people leading our churches who are functioning in a priestly role and, with the heightening awareness of spiritual warfare, in a kingly role. What we are in need of are those with a prophetic spirit and word.

In the New Testament the prophet moved in a team or out of a team. The ministries that God has given are a sort of construction team to help initiate, oversee, motivate, teach and train the church, as well as seeing it enlarged through witness and declaration. One of my major concerns is that many who claim to be prophetic are not accountable to any of the ministries listed in Ephesians 4. They are not in teams. Even the Lone Ranger had Tonto! Sometimes isolation creates misunderstanding; misunderstanding leads to mistrust. Without trust progress is impossible.

Recently I was reminded that almost twenty years ago I spoke in the West Country in what was then a small group. I was told the title of my talk was 'To whom are you accountable and how are you getting on with your partner?' Teaming is important. In the Old Testament if you claimed to speak on behalf of the Almighty, and it was later seen that you were most certainly not, you were stoned to death. It's a very serious thing to claim to be an ambassador for the greatest personality in the universe, purporting to have messages from him when they came from a heavy cheese supper, a vivid imagination, or a less noble motive. If the British Ambassador to America dared to communicate messages to the American government on behalf of the Prime Minister, when he knew nothing of such messages, there would be international chaos. Accountability is vital!

The big 'three'

Money, sex and pride will alter the shape of the church to come! They look for loners to subvert. There will be times when the prophet can be forgiven for feeling, 'I and only I am left.' Those with prophetic ministry are always in danger of making their prophetic ministry the truth. 'We know in part and we prophesy in part' (1 Cor 13:9). As my friend John Noble puts it so well, 'We all have a valid perspective on almost everything, but it may not be the truth.' Experience shows that it rarely is. Prophetic ministry must not be reduced to mere perspective. But that is where accountability comes in. It starts with a desire to be accountable and then proceeds by looking for peers (not lesser 'yes' people) to whom we can become accountable. It does not start by people demanding we be accountable to them, but rather we adopt an attitude of accountability ourselves. That in itself will act as a balance when we claim to speak on behalf of God.

I am kept happy for days on end when I hear that prophecies or words of knowledge God has given me have been wonderfully fulfilled. A few days before beginning this chapter I was in Gloucestershire and prayed and prophesied over a number of people at the close of the meeting. As I wrote I received a letter from the leader of that group of churches telling me that he had 'raised eyebrows' when I told one young man, 'You are about to receive promotion from the Lord.' The very next day he was offered an executive post in a nationally networked campaign. Around that time God also gave me a word for a graphic designer/illustrator who once worked for British Telecom and thankfully got rid of Busby! He was also drawn upon as a consultant to help package companies, give them a sense of identity and purpose and talked with management about how they should be promoted. I sensed God was asking me to prophesy over him in front of several hundred people. In my vision I saw him sitting at a Board table. His godly wisdom, insight and integrity were touching the lives of key people in the world of business. He came up to me afterwards a d hugged me, but was speechless. Little did I know, as I found out s veral days later through a mutual friend, that he'd been somewhat disenchanted with what he was doing because he felt his business perspectives were ignored and his insights not taken note of, even though he was being paid to give them. That very week the United Nations contacted him, asking him if he would fly to America 'as soon as possible' as they needed his perspectives, insight and skill!

Shaping prophets and churches

The need for prophets in *team* ministry is obvious. The prophet's oratory and often sparkling insights can walk off with the hearts of the entire congregation. The shape of the prophet can determine the shape of the church to come. Their words and our response have immense importance. There is an interesting study for those inclined to take it up on our behalf. Would certain things have happened in Bible days if the prophets hadn't prophesied they would? An interesting study indeed! God spoke and things came to pass. If God hadn't spoken would they have come to pass anyway? Prophetic ministry will see the church purified and empowered. It is interesting that most denominational churches doubt or completely fail to acknowledge prophetic ministry. Those who don't fit in with the system of things, or challenge the system of things, are seen as immature or irrational. 'No prophet is welcome in his home town' (Lk 4:24, NASB). I might add 'denomination'

Recognising prophets

If prophets are so vital in shaping up the church, how do you recognise them? They don't all look the same. Elijah wore high-class clothes; John the Baptist animal skins. Isaiah was from a palace, whereas Amos from among the sheep. Elijah was called 'a man of fire', whereas Jeremiah was positively timid. God chooses prophets. Pastors and bishops don't! They don't exist merely to prophesy what the status quo and leaders desire. Prophets must be acquainted with the eternal word of Scripture. They will influence lives with the 'now' word of God. God's word is always relevant, but he chooses people to make that relevant word connect. Amos tells us the Lord 'reveals his secret counsel to his servants the prophets' (Amos 3:7).

The trouble is, the prophets are looking into the future and often spoiling our present-day fun. They continually demand that we get in line with God's revealed will in Scripture. To me the Scriptures are like a vast ocean of water and prophecy is but a cupful of water. But a cupful of water can save a life and getting the cup to the need is what often matters.

Near to where I live there is a grand property, Painshill House. Its gardens are currently being renovated and restored. Prince Charles and the Duchess of York are making several visits to oversee its development. A long time ago the house was turned into apartments. A while back the owner of one of the apartments decided to knock down a wall in the basement to see what was there. To his astonishment he found thousands of bottles of wine that had been stored there for many years. The cellar had once been a reservoir of enjoyment for those who were partial to a glass of wine. But for some strange reason it had been bricked up. The prophet will often act as a door (or a sledge-hammer!), not only making God's word accessible, but making God's resources available to those shut off from that supply.

But the local church cannot live on prophetic ministry alone. It will stagger from one almighty revelation to another. In the charismatic movement as a whole, the level of prophecy is appallingly low. Hardly the stuff that will change the direction of a meeting, never mind a city or a nation. Prophets, once recognised, must be encouraged to wait on God with their gift. They either serve God, the leadership, the church as a whole or those outside the church. Indeed they should be encouraged to travel the area or network and have influence in those churches. They don't need to be full time to do that.

The problems of prophecy

1. Unfulfilled prophecy

Most of the Book of Revelation is unfulfilled. Indeed, without the Holy Spirit we cannot understand what John saw. Futuristic charts available in most Christian bookshops are usually the result of hard work, vain imagination and hardly a thread of revelation. Study and revelation are vital. The vast majority of what Peter said on the Day of Pentecost from Joel is still unfulfilled. 'This' was indeed 'that', but it wasn't *all* of that! Heroes of faith died without prophecy being fulfilled. It is damaging to reject prophecy—especially from proven prophets. You cannot resist God's word and remain sane.

2. *False prophecy*

Here are three tests: (a) If the predicted event doesn't happen when it was supposed to, it was not of God—God is not a liar (Deut 18:22). (b) If the prophecy denies God or Christ it is false (Deut 13). (c) If a prophecy contradicts what God has already commanded it is false (1 Kings 13:11–34; Rev 22:18–19). Again I urge caution in jumping to false conclusions.

3. *Revoked prophecy*

God is moved by what people do and how they respond to his word and his servants. Jonah prophesied destruction on Nineveh, but the people repented and God did not destroy them. Moses prayed for Israel when God was about to destroy them and God shelved his judgement. Much of prophecy is conditional.

However, we are not to be the playthings of the words of those who claim to speak on behalf of God. We have the witness of the Holy Spirit, the history, lessons and values of Scripture and the ability to respond as Mary did. When the angel prophesied over her, it was far too wonderful to believe or understand. 'May it be to me as you have said,' was her response (Lk 1:38). So often we have to say, 'Lord, if this is your word, be it unto me according to your word.' Equally we are allowed to say, 'And if it's not, let it just evaporate.' Even when we are not sure about things we can say, 'God, we are not sure whether this is your word or not, we are unclear, so in your infinite mercy please bring this word to us from another source at another time to confirm.' We are not doing it out of unbelief but out of care for our own integrity and those we are responsible for.

The prophets are speaking! Networks of people are responding. The shape of the church is changing! God is wanting to accelerate that work through his word.

God's prophetic thrust

So what is the main thrust of 'what God is doing' in the nation (that well-worn and oft-abused phrase)?

1. A massive strategy of church planting

Every church that is relatively healthy must be planning to plant and therefore divide. For the way to multiplication is division. The mega-church with its mega-meetings is fine, but when the mega-meeting *is* the church, it's not the church. It's just a meeting. Large events such as March for Jesus, Greenbelt, Spring Harvest or Billy Graham Crusades are wonderful. They raise the visibility of the Christian church. And visibility is vital if we're going to affect the mindset of the nation. But in the final analysis, it is Christians in our villages, towns and cities who matter. If the former gives visibility, the latter will give credibility. If we are rarely at home because we are either at work or at church we will never affect our area.

Sadly, in many places, uniformity, predictable conformity and mediocrity are seen as virtues. Indeed, almost signs of progress. These churches don't plant. For to church-plant needs vision, training and leadership development. This leaves no room for a policy of pastoral maintenance, consolidation and stagnation, self-indulgence or self-sufficiency.

Teenagers, once attracted, must be envisioned and trained for leadership. I started what is now known as the Cobham Christian Fellowship in 1970 when I was twenty-five years old. Much of my character needed shaping, areas of my life needed adjustment, my communication skills had not developed and I was unable to handle many things that I do with relative ease today. But if the newer churches fail to attract these raw teenagers it is the beginning of the end. We all grow old and die! If we do not give them room to develop, responsibilities to take on and opportunity for success and mistakes, we shall lose them as they become frustrated out of their minds. They will either settle into inflexibility or redirect their energies into business or the home.

Where to plant? That is often the question. Our policy at Pioneer is simple. We only go to an area of a town or city where there are no churches currently taking (or planning to take) the gospel to every household in that area. It matters not to us whether the church is Calvinistic, traditional, Pentecostal or charismatic. If they are evangelising and building Christian community we are not needed. If they are not, then another church who *will* reach the area with the gospel *must* be planted. Jesus said that when we take the gospel to the ends of the earth—'then the end will come' (Mt 24:14). It's easy. If we want to bring an end to this rotten, corrupt and unjust age we must take the gospel wherever we can. Britain and the rest of Europe is one of the most unevangelised areas of the world! But even if you're reading this in Australia, New Zealand, the USA or South Africa, you have plenty to do!

2. *A release of people into ministry*

It has been said that there are three sorts of people in the church: There are those who make things happen. There are those who help make things happen. And then there are the vast majority who wonder what on earth is happening!

People are the church's greatest resource. We are not all orators, worship leaders, pastors or indeed house-group leaders. But in so many churches it is the committed core who are doing almost everything. 'If you want to get a job done ask a busy person' still holds true. But the committed core must train others into commitment to Christ and his purposes so that throughout the body of Christ we have a committed, caring and mature resource.

There is of course the issue of women in ministry and leadership which I know is a very controversial one. I do not wish to address that in this chapter as Christine Noble has done so further on. But we have been like an army fighting with one arm tied behind our back with 50% of our battle resources stuck at home. Whatever our views are on women in leadership, eldership or apostleship—women in ministry and leadership are all over the Bible. They need to be seen as a resource of energy, insight, intuition, plain commonsense and godly anointing.

I am not here talking about merely giving men, women or the young a 'chance' to try themselves out—to have a bash or give them a bit of experience. I am talking about training, oversight, encouragement and direction. A clear brief about what to do and how to do it. When they look after the tools we give them, we can give them their own tools, their own business and their own responsibilities. The commercial world that just gives junior staff opportunities without training, direction and understanding will be bankrupt within months. I see many inexperienced people who are merely 'having a go' return home depressed and dejected without any forum for feedback, encouragement or correction. They operate with no goal in view. Everything we do should be evaluated in the light of our goal.

We don't need to be leaders to release each other into useful-ness in creative evangelism or pastoral care, prophetic ministry or administration, music or the miraculous, healing or deliverance, prayer or intercession, ministries among the young or the elderly, the single or the married, the sick or the unemployed. Some people need to be released to make money to invest in the kingdom. They should be encouraged to settle with God (before they start) what they are going to give him rather than make up a sum as they go along. This brings me to the third point.

3. Release of finance into God's work

Most of the New Churches teach tithing. Some as an Old Testament principle and others simply as a good principle. But just because we have given our pound in ten does not mean we can switch off with a 'we've done our bit' philosophy. There needs to be central giving for the central 'family account' and commitments. There are full-time leaders to support, the administration, base, publications, gifts to be given to the needy—this is best centralised. But there must also be freedom to continue to give to the poor, and people outside the church, by individuals. People should be encouraged to support their leaders and families. Central giving to the exclusion of personal giving can cause us to look upon tithes or regular giving as a bill along with mortgage, electricity and gas. However, if everyone gave as they 'felt led' I am sure the church would have a dose of 'felt-led poisoning'! That is not how God has ordained it. Money in the Old and New Testament was laid at the feet of authority.

We may as well face a problem here and now. The more a person, or a family, or a church has, the more 'worldly' they are tempted to become. Worldliness does not consist of what you've got, but has to do with an attitude of heart. To have a beaten-up Hillman Minx insured for 'any driver' is one thing; having the latest model insured for anyone to drive is something quite different! Loaning our rented flat or small terraced house to a needy family for a while is one thing, but loaning our well-decorated and comfortably furnished detached house is another. Wesley found precisely the same problem. He preached to the poor and it wasn't long before gambling, excessive drinking and smoking were abandoned by the converts. Budgets were kept, people had more money to spend on themselves. They began to give to God and his work, but because of the sowing and reaping cycle they were then blessed with finances both naturally and supernaturally. Money was saved, property purchased and the standard of living went up. I want to make it clear that poverty is not what God is aiming for and should not be what the Christian is aiming for. But neither is wealth.

However, the next generation (our children) will have to face an even greater problem than most of us. I live in Surrey and in 1985 an average house cost £75,000. In 1988 that house was worth £150,000! Personally, I would like another forty years before my wife and I go to meet the Lord. By by the year 2000 I will be in my mid-fifties—about the same time both my parents died. If we died then, our three sons would inherit all that money.

My wife Anona and I started with nothing. We rented property, had no central heating for years, took no holiday for seven years and I don't remember buying any new clothes for the first few years of our marriage. I lived by faith (nearly died by it, actually) for another seven years. In short we proved God. Without those experiences I wouldn't have the same faith in God that I have now. Faith grows. I believed God for a weekly income, then for a monthly income and then a yearly income. I believed God for massive sums of money for projects which were impossible. I've believed God to provide me for income with staff and personnel when there was nothing on the horizon. The person who hasn't trusted God for a meal should never trust God for a car or home.

Anona and I have written our wills so that benefit comes to the Pioneer Trust and its work in evangelism, church planting, March for Jesus, Support for the Jubilee Campaign, ACET the AIDS care initiative, and overseas work. Of course we want to see our sons benefit from our hard work, but the newer churches and denominational evangelicals involved in charismatic renewal are in great danger of increasing their standard of living, becoming detached from the world of the poor and the lower middle classes (particularly in the South of England and beyond) without extending the kingdom one iota. Many of us need to settle now what we want to leave to Christian work, evangelistic and church-planting ministries and Christian charities, and what we are going to leave to our children and friends.

Mosques are being completed at the rate of one a fortnight in Britain. Millions of pounds are being invested into the UK by Muslims. Collective strategies are being initiated in other countries. Their people are giving to see the Muslim kingdom extended. If we are going to be effective and cover our nation with the gospel it will need resources and funds.

I confess I have been disappointed where I have seen 'Spirit-filled Christians' inherit money from parents, relatives or friends. In one instance, the inheritors took a couple of friends on holiday to Spain, while the rest went on a brand new car, an enlarged kitchen, another holiday abroad and a little in the bank for a rainy day. I am pleased they had such a good time. I am sure they deserved the money. But the kingdom of God was not extended, not a soul got saved and the church didn't benefit at all. In another case a very large sum of money was left a couple, one tenth was put into the local church and the rest (a vast sum) was spent on property. The bill had been paid, God had got his tenth and that was it.

I often get invitations from third world countries to minister among them. We take a team and equipment, but the host countries have little way of paying for air fares and accommodation. Some of the teams I take look upon a trip abroad with great anticipation. They can afford an air fare once every two or three years. But it is impossible to take three or four trips a year out of family funds. So often the training of the church and the evangelism of nations is held up while people are substantially increasing their standards of living without thought to the kingdom. We are in great need of godly men and women with a vision to release hundreds, thousands and even hundreds of thousands of pounds into the work of God. One Pioneer church gave us a gift that started our TIE Teams (Training In Evangelism). They are now self-financing. But we needed to pump in prime finances to get things going, and as a result hundreds have been brought into the kingdom.

What we do with our money will shape the church, but sadly money often shapes us. It feeds our desire for comfort and ease, leading to apathy and self-indulgence. Without standing together and sharing our resources the one thing I can do by myself is fail. But together, investing resources in one another, we can see the kingdom of God extended and the gospel reach the ends of the earth and cover our nations.

4. Nurtured relationships

Every relationship of value and worth must be constantly nurtured. In the business of church planting, releasing finances, shaping up ministries and pioneering on behalf of others, relationships must not be ignored or taken for granted.

At the heart of the Godhead is relationships. The Trinity is the only model we have for relationships—the three-in-one, a family or community. They do not have to discuss things to come to unity. They are intrinsic oneness. The Father does not know more than the Son (now), the Son is not more powerful than the Spirit. But the Holy Spirit pays Jesus the highest accolade and Jesus pays his Father the highest accolade and they bring glory to one another. There is order within their relationship, they are co-powerful, co-equal in knowledge and understanding. One does not move without the full approval and commitment of the other. What a model! The job is never put before the relationship, the task never erodes their love and commitment to one another. The new dimensions Jesus moved in within the space-time world never eroded his faithfulness to his heavenly Father. Relationships were nurtured and honoured.

The three major issues evangelicals must face are racism, sexism and nationalism. It was John Perkins who said, 'If white people can move beyond their guilt, and black people beyond blame, we can create beautiful, evangelistic, social and economic alternatives in the poor communities.' We need each other.

It is interesting to note that when Roman Catholicism emerged it taught that sin should be confessed to a priest. When Protestantism was birthed they said it was necessary only to confess wrongs to God. Then up popped Freud, who told us there were no sins to confess at all; proving that the further we get away from one another the more prone we are to deception, heresy and harm.

If we have no time to pray with each other then we are truly too busy. If we have no time together to enjoy food and drink, we are shallow. For as C S Lewis stated, pleasure is God's invention not the devil's. Praying with each other as well as eating and drinking together involves believing the best of one another. It creates a forum of love and care, and harmonises energies, enabling us to continue in our work more successfully. It leaves little room for rumour and enemy activity. We must not take who and what we have for granted, but nurture, bless and nourish those around us whenever we can and however we can.

Friendship and fellowship bless the soul and 'calm the troubled breast'. In this way we shall be among the most hard-working, able, morally disciplined and sensitive in the land. This can only enhance the work we have to do. It will keep us clean inside, and cleanliness on the inside will help shape the church on the outside.

The tongue is the revealer of what is inside of us. Speech between friends and colleagues is the interaction between the seen and the unseen. Relationships will protect us as we engage more fully in spiritual warfare. By God's grace we have chosen to change our allegiance. Satan is not ambivalent about us. He hates us! He hates our answered prayers, healed bodies, changed lives. He hates the fact that we have become agents of change, communicators of reconciliation and that we love our Lord Jesus who is able to forgive sinners and deliver the demonised. The person nurturing relationships is the person protected. The person in isolation is the person open to attack.

The challenge of a new beginning

Disappointment with the past and nothing but despair for the future form the curse of millions in the UK. But Scripture and the Holy Spirit help us to see things in a new light. What appears to have been defeat is victory. We see this at Calvary. We shall see it in our own time, despite the declining church attendance, downright heresy among church leaders and the reproach of Christ's name. God will provide for us a new beginning with new light. This book is about that beginning and that light.

But this 'new light' is not at all new. It is wrapped up in Christ and his kingdom. It is at the very centre of our being. It must be at the centre of our families and churches. The King and his kingdom will ultimately determine the shape of the church to come. God is not a celestial tyrant. His mercies are from everlasting to everlasting. Faith enables us to see what is not obvious.

So we shall all answer one way or another, both with our lives and resources, the question, 'How do we break the mould of go-nowhere Christianity?' But we need to ask one another the question, 'What if God answers our prayers? What if he pours his Spirit out, the church grows, our influence is enlarged and the nation is blessed in answer to many prayers?' We should not ask, 'What shall I do if I do not reach my goals?' but rather, 'What should I do if I do?' We move towards what we respect.

Indeed, where we go to from here on has much to do with what we respect. It could be smallness or greatness, getting or giving, success or failure, usefulness or comfort, positive action or negative reaction, illicit sex or faithful love.

We are an addicted society. Either to drugs or to sex, money or property, cars, clothing or independency. There is an obvious breakdown of morality and ethics, family respect and authority. What do we respect? The negative, sarcastic authority deriding? The spirit of the age or biblical values? Your human spirit will also determine the shape of the church to come.

Either way (whatever shape we're in), we shall have to face the increasing problems of drugs, alcoholism, divorce, child abuse, AIDS, gene splitting, artificial insemination, premarital and extra-marital sex, and the results of lesbianism and homosexuality. We shall have to face it first in our own families, which is going to be quite a shock to some Christians reading this chapter. You don't know what your sons and daughters will turn out to be like and simply wielding a biblical stick over them generally produces the thing we fear will happen. It's impossible to grow and flourish under constant disapproval. Then we shall have to face it in our schools, places of work and even our churches.

We must shape up! Most of those early disciples had to deal with this very question, 'How do *we* break the mould?' after Jesus left them and ascended into heaven. The issues they faced were somewhat different, but no less real. We benefit from 2,000 years of history and traditional church values.

But the future belongs to us because it has been given to Christ. We must invest our lives and ministries in the next generation, for they may face a tougher job than we. We must pray for our future, we shall be spending the rest of our time there!

A people radical, prophetic, investing in others, sharing resources, nurturing relationships—all deeply affecting the shape of the church to come.

I am a generalist, but I have surrounded myself with specialists. The following chapters are from Pioneer team members who are out in the field, not in from the battle writing cosy paragraphs with binoculars in their hands! May they help you to 'break the mould' of any traditional form of Christianity that balks at doing the job in hand: impacting the world with the gospel of Christ.

2

Apostles and Prophets

John Noble

John Noble is Chairman of the Charismatic Leaders' Conference, is an advisor to Christian leaders and organisations, especially to Gerald Coates, and conducts a wide travelling speaking ministry. He has written several books. He and his wife Christine have five children.

Apostles and prophets have exploded onto the church scene in the last couple of decades—a sure sign, in my opinion, that we are drawing to the close of the age. In the United Kingdom there are maybe a score or more so-called apostolic teams in the New Church networks, with estimates of around a thousand related churches, and there are similar team initiatives and church-planting programmes developing within some of the denominations. If neglect of these ministries in the early church marked a decline in spirituality and growth, then their restoration today will surely mean life and health for God's people—even though, as is almost always the case, with the increase of maturity we can expect an increase of persecution. Renewal seldom progresses without mistakes and excesses which the enemy uses to bring disenchantment, so that the truth is often rejected along with the failure. If we are to avoid hiccups and delays we must endeavour to understand the proper purpose and function, in our culture and setting, of these gifts which are foundational to church nurture and expansion.

During the emerging period we can expect to see false apostles motivated by ambition, greed and sometimes by Satan himself and, by contrast but still not the genuine article, sincere but misguided saints who are caught up in the excitement of the awakening. Nevertheless, we must not react, but try to identify, release and respect those chosen and gifted by Jesus for this important work. For centuries, because Christians had been fooled into believing apostles and prophets were for the infant church alone, or perhaps because we despised these ministries, we have been guilty of jerry-building. We have put up structures and created networks which, although not without their blessings, have seldom stood the test of time and have never quite achieved what was in Jesus' heart. As one friend of mine used to say about his early years as a Christian, 'I spent my first seventeen years taking short cuts, but I was no nearer my destination at the end.' Sadly, it has been the same in the church for so long, but now is the time and the opportunity for change.

If we are to acknowledge and encourage apostles and prophets, and benefit from their wisdom and the teams they spawn, we need to grasp the full spectrum of the God-given burdens which make up their calling and commission. It is my firm conviction that a worldwide network of recognition and friendship will develop which will bring cohesion and stability to the church, and lead to co-operation across cultural and national divides. For if Jesus is the head of the church, the church must be seen to be under his authority, and that authority will never endorse independence, party spirit or competition. So, what are the prime concerns of apostles and prophets?

Why have apostles and prophets today?

There has been a great deal of talk around the subject of apostles, prophets and apostolic teams, and most charismatic Christians, particularly from what the press have dubbed the 'New Churches', would readily come up with answers to my question. These would almost invariably include church planting and maintenance, prophecy, signs and wonders and leadership development all topping the list. Of course these are important aspects of their work, but there are other vital yet more neglected areas which are also keys to enabling the church to fulfil her obligations in terms of reaching the world in our generation. Without attempting to produce an exhaustive list or a biblical justification which would be unrealistic in one short chapter, I'd like to highlight some of these concerns, for this will most certainly determine our effectiveness in building church and fulfilling the Great Commission. First, and perhaps most importantly, apostles and prophets will be guardians and purveyors of truth.

Evangelical Christians, particularly British evangelicals, have prided themselves as being defenders of the faith. In fact, this has turned out to be defending a form of doctrine which for centuries has totally missed, or worse rejected, whole areas of vital truth— the most notable, but by no means the only area, being the supernatural work of the Holy Spirit in the church. Christ-appointed ministries will not be locked in to traditional dogmatic boundaries, nor will they be tossed around by every wind of doctrine. They will hold fast to the truth as it is revealed to them by Jesus. This will not contradict Scripture, but it will involve them in paradox.

For example, at times they will oppose religious structures which threaten a work of the Holy Spirit, and in another situation they will relate to, and encourage, Christians within those same structures and traditions. They will know beyond question that the truth is not finally to be found in tenets or creeds, necessary though it may be for teachers to wrestle with the difficulties of expressing truth in them, but they will portray truth as a Person— Jesus, and show that truth can only be properly understood through a relationship with him. As with Jesus himself, truth manifested through apostles and prophets will never be harsh and destructive in its dealings with other believers, but always 'seasoned with grace'. In today's renewal this will provide a climate for co-operation without compromise, for recognising the work of Jesus in the lives of fellow believers with whom, as yet, we are not 'united in the faith'. Not everyone is able to handle the tensions involved in this. It requires a special grace which I have observed among some denominational leaders like Father Tom Forrest. Revd Donald English, Canon Michael Harper and many others who are pioneers.

Unity in the Spirit

The culmination of Jesus' burden must surely have been released in his priestly prayer prior to going to the cross. He cried out to the Father from the depths of his heart for three things: that his glory might be given to the church; that the church might be one, and that the world might believe. Jesus was referring to exactly the same glory he received from the Father and exactly the same unity he enjoyed with his Father, which resulted in men and women believing in him wherever he went. Clearly there is a link between these three things: no glory—no unity; no unity—no one believes. It is also clear that Jesus was asking his Father for glory and unity in the church before his return to earth, 'so that the world may believe'. After his second coming it would be too late for believing.

It is inconceivable that apostles and prophets appointed by the Lord should not share this, his greatest concern. To adopt an attitude which says, 'I'll get on with what God's given me to do; it's too much of a hindrance trying to relate to other Christians,' may be justified for some saints under certain circumstances, but it cannot be an attitude which is entertained by ministries called to be imitators of Christ and shepherds of his flock. David the psalmist understood this when, in Psalm 133, he declared, 'How good and pleasant it is when brothers live together in unity! . . . for there the Lord bestows his blessing.' Living together in unity demands a response from the Father. In Ephesians 4 Paul, in his apostolic role, calls the church to keep the unity given to them by the Spirit. In such an atmosphere of peace among God's people which will be promoted by apostles, Christ will raise up other apostles and prophets who will prepare and equip the church for service. This will demand a maturity beyond anything we have seen in recent years and will result in a greater 'unity of faith' and 'the whole measure of the fullness of Christ' visible in the church. Only such a church with the whole Christ released within her, is properly equipped to give opportunity for the whole world to believe. I am not talking here about localised revival or mission, but all peoples of all nations being confronted by glory in the church at one and the same time!

An exciting prospect, but let's get back to the facts. The reality is that it will take the same kind of sacrificial love as was seen in Jesus to achieve this, and that means suffering. Suffering apostles and prophets, who can uphold and sustain a suffering church in a world which is bent on destroying that church, are a necessary part of God's end-time strategy.

Apostles and prophets will know suffering

Even a superficial glance through the Acts of the Apostles will reveal that a large part of what it takes to be an apostle or a prophet entails suffering. This should not come as a surprise to us, but it is not something we hear a great deal about in the West. The subject of prosperity is much nearer to our hearts. Although it is not often voiced, there is an 'I love Christ but hate the church' attitude under the surface, in the lives of many Christians. We see the weaknesses in the church; we have been hurt and let down by the church; through pride and in-fighting the church has failed in her task; even the world is disillusioned with the church; but in spite of all this and more, Jesus loved the church and gave himself for her. If apostles and prophets have been truly raised up by Jesus, they will carry the same love and willingness to give themselves for Jesus' body on earth. If Jesus has committed himself to work through the church, then how can his deputies do any less?

Jeremiah is an example to today's apostles and prophets for, in spite of their terrible backsliding and waywardness, he loved God's people. 'Since my people are crushed, I am crushed,' he cried. 'Oh that my head were a spring of water and my eyes a fountain of tears! I would cry day and night for the slain of my people.' Jeremiah, like Jesus, wept when he saw the sin and hypocrisy at the very centre of God's chosen ones. Hard words to be delivered? Yes! Calls for repentance? Yes! Captivity and punishment prophesied? Yes! But stop loving God's people, stop hoping and believing for change, stop being willing to sacrifice for them? Never! For Christ is sold out to his people and, therefore, so are we.

Apostles and prophets know that we can't make it alone. They know that, while salvation may start with the individual, it ends with the corporate. Jesus is not coming back for a motley crew of independent wanderers—but for a nation held together by a common life and identity in him. No matter how long we have to wait or how much we have to suffer, in the end Jesus will have a healthy church 'without spot or wrinkle' to carry his image and manifest his power on the earth.

In the early church, unity of Spirit was to be maintained. Today, before we can maintain it, we must discover it. Because of the suspicions and divisions which have accumulated and multiplied over centuries among Christians, a great part of the apostolic and prophetic work in the Western world where Christianity has been around for a while, will involve reconciliation. Untangling the mare's-nest of dissension which has grown up, as well as tackling current conflict, will be no easy task. It will mean going back to the Gospels to discover what Jesus taught us, the absolute basic essentials of church life. These are twofold and cut through all secondary issues and man-made traditions: first, in Matthew 16, Jesus spoke of a revelation and relationship to himself as being the foundation on which the church is built. Second, in Matthew 18, he made it clear that right relationships to one another are also necessary to maintain the church and release power, through her prayers. Only those who 'agree' can hope to receive the promise 'anything you ask for will be done'. The enormity of this commission is such that only ministries that have a genuine call from Jesus and have heard his declaration, 'I will build my church', will survive, let alone succeed.

Many years ago, while meditating in Ezekiel 37, I saw the bones of God's people strewn throughout the valley of death and destruction. There were Methodist bones and Anglican bones, Baptist bones and Brethren bones, Roman Catholic bones and Salvation Army bones. No house church bones were there then because at that time we didn't exist—but there are plenty now! I heard the question, 'Can these bones live?' I have little expectation for such a miracle, but found myself saying, 'You know, Lord.' Today almost every denomination has godly and, mostly, Spirit-filled men or women at the helm, and there is an ever-increasing number of local churches coming alive in the Spirit too. What a relief it was to me, against the chilling background of decline and decay, to hear Jesus proclaim with total confidence, 'I will build my church and the gates of hell shall not prevail against it!'

Apostles and prophets will be aware of their total dependence upon Jesus—if he doesn't do it, it won't get done! They also share his confidence in the face of what appear to be totally impossible circumstances—because he said he'd do it, it will be done! Like Haggai and Zechariah of old, they look at the dereliction of the temple and smile because they know who the builder is. When they see the 'mighty mountain' of apathy, formalism, hypocrisy and confusion which stands in the way of the rebuilding, they declare, 'The one who laid the foundation will also complete it! They are not deterred by the sight of a heap of rubble, but simply get on with that part of the renovation work to which they have been assigned.

Mutual dependence

Finally, end-time apostles and prophets will not simply urge others to go forward together, they will go forward together themselves While they may have a particular calling to a particular work to which they are dedicated, they will recognise their need of one another. As in Nehemiah's day different tribes and family groupings were allocated different sections of the wall to repair, so it is in today's work of restoration. However, we are all working under the same authority and building the same walls. Not all teamwork takes place in cricket or football teams, playing together at the same time in the same place. Some is more akin to the athletics team, where each one plays in a different event at a different time, but they're all on the same side. Whatever the setting, team spirit, affirmation, correction, support and co-operation wherever possible are always to be encouraged.

I am most grateful to the Lord for recently placing Christine and me alongside my friend Gerald Coates in the Pioneer team, just when they are in a period of blessing and expansion. They're a wonderful bunch of people and, I believe, are set for great things in God. So much is opening up to them at different levels in society, in the media and in the international scene. Nevertheless, successful though Gerald and his team are, we're only a tiny part of what God wants to do in our nation and across the world. We would be fools to believe that we can achieve anything but smallness without the rest of our brothers and sisters who share the vision of the world for Christ and Christ for the world. Like Pioneer, more and more house church leaders and their teams are forsaking their parochial boundaries to see how they can co-operate together. Yet still there are those teams, individual ministries and churches, who are either living in glorious ignorance or who are determined to do their own thing, come what may. We don't have to lose our identity or compromise our God-given distinctives to get alongside the apostles and prophets whom Jesus is giving to us at this point in the history of his church. So, let us find our place in the body and let us go forward, in the flow of the Holy Spirit. Forward—together!

3

Prophets and Prophecy

Martin Scott

Martin Scott led the Pioneer People, Cobham for several years, before working in the Pioneer South and West of London region, having input into churches particularly at a faith and vision level. He is also in growing demand as a speaker alongside his healing ministry. Martin is married to Sue and they have two young children, Benjamin and Judith.

He is the author of Prophecy in the Church *in the Pioneer Perspective series (Word (UK) 1992).*

The Holy Spirit was poured out in a most dramatic way upon a certain group of people. The spokesperson for the group stood up and explained that something new had begun. Those who listened to him were witnessing the beginning of a new era—one of its hallmarks would be the widespread distribution of the gift of prophecy. That morning in Jerusalem, Peter boldly stated that this experience was the fulfilment of Joel's prophecy (Acts 2:16). The 'last days' had finally arrived and throughout that period prophecy would continue to feature.

During the Old Testament era prophecy had mainly been restricted to those who had been appointed to the prophetic office. Now Peter explained that prophecy was linked to a liberal outpouring of the Holy Spirit and could be experienced by anyone, regardless of age or gender. In fact Peter added some extra words to his quote from Joel which further underlined the centrality of prophecy within this new experience. He added the words 'and they will prophesy' (Acts 2:18), so removing any doubt that prophecy was simply an insignificant side-effect to the outpouring of the Holy Spirit.

Prophecy is described as one of the manifestations of the Holy Spirit (1 Cor 12:10) and should release the manifest (almost tangible) presence of God. Prophecy brings the word of God in a very direct way as it communicates in precise terms what God is currently saying to any given situation or person. It might not reveal everything, but the effect of being exposed to prophetic revelation and insight is to feel that God has significantly spoken into the whole situation. We see this particularly in John 4 which records Jesus' conversation with the woman at the well. Through revelation he spoke accurately about her marital status. This clear word concerned one specific area of her life, but she felt that Jesus had told her everything she had ever done (see John 4:17–18, 39).

In our own church we have experienced God speak many times through prophecy. On occasions the message simply expressed his love and encouraged us to pursue our current course. Such prophecies are important particularly during times of doubt or hardship. At other times we have had specific words which have warned of things to come; things which could not have been known by any element of human guesswork. On yet other occasions prophecies have been given which have spoken of new things that God is doing, and as a result the whole course of the church has moved forward with a strategic change of direction. Prophecy has become a vital experience for us and we have seen individuals and corporate groups changed through the release of the prophetic word.

Prophecy is a dynamic tool of the Holy Spirit but, as with all tools, if it is abused it can become something quite dangerous and destructive. For example, in 1948 there was a very strong prophetic movement which originated in Canada called the Latter Rain Movement. It would appear that it began with a genuine outpouring of the Holy Spirit, but evidence of abuse in certain areas soon became apparent. Prophecy was being used to manipulate and control other individuals. So much so that some of the main Pentecostal denominations in the USA banned the use of personal prophecy because of such unfortunate experiences. There is a new emphasis on prophecy today—some would even talk of a 'prophetic movement'—and it is important that we do not repeat the mistakes of the past resulting in prophecy being despised because of bad experiences.

Genuine prophetic gifts are being restored and in such times it is easy to make mistakes. In the light of this, I wish to address two important areas. First, I want to suggest some guidelines which will help us weigh prophecy, and secondly I will put forward some pointers with regard to the development of prophetic ministry.

'The others should weigh carefully' (1 Cor 14:29)

Prophecy must be weighed, otherwise abuse can soon enter and the true gift become discredited. Those who prophesy must be prepared to receive comments on what they have to say. No prophecy should automatically be treated as true and accurate simply because of the speaker's reputation. The weighing of prophecy is vital if churches are to benefit from this gift.

Obviously prophecy needs to accord with the teaching of Scripture and should uplift Jesus. When a word conflicts with the above principles then we know that we can safely reject it. Such a word is easy to 'weigh carefully' and we can be thankful that such words are few and far between. The requirement to weigh prophecy highlights the importance of teaching Scripture within the church, so that new ideas and concepts are not merely accepted as the latest revelation from heaven.

A word which contradicts Scripture or leads us away from Jesus is simple to deal with. A more difficult problem arises when a prophecy is given which cannot be clearly weighed against the biblical data. For example, how should a leadership weigh a word which instructs them to plant out a new congregation in a town fifteen miles away? It is clearly not unbiblical, in the light of the

Great Commission, to plant churches, but on what basis should they accept or reject such a word as being from God? Again, by way of example, Jehoshaphat in 2 Chronicles 18 is faced with 400 prophets saying that he should move forward in one direction, but the prophet Micaiah is prophesying the exact opposite. What principles can we use to help us in such situations?

Before we look at some principles that can be employed, I would like to throw another complicating factor into the mix! This additional issue concerns the accuracy or otherwise of the content of a prophetic word. Life would be easy if we were to accept all words which were accurate and reject any words which could be proved to contain inaccuracies. However, prophecy cannot be weighed by this simple procedure. Paul faced an interesting situation in Philippi where a true word was proclaimed, but he discerned the source as being a demonic spirit (Acts 16:16–18). Today we might have been tempted to build the church around this woman and her contacts! So even if a word is factually accurate we will find that this one criterion alone will be insufficient in helping us to weigh it adequately.

The converse is also true—if a prophecy is inaccurate in places we might still be able to receive the word as a whole, but would then need to throw out the parts which were inaccurate. (This could well be the situation that Paul addresses in 1 Thessalonians 5:19–21 when he says that we are not to 'treat prophecies with contempt' but are to 'test everything' and 'hold on to the good'.) However much it might offend our analytical minds it is vital that we realise our first response is to weigh all prophetic words at a spiritual level. Inaccuracies do sometimes occur in prophecy when someone speaks out a true word from God, but either through insecurity or lack of discipline adds their own interpretation to it. In such cases our responsibility is to weigh the 'spirit' of the word so that we can receive the revelation which God is giving and then discard any errors in the communication.

I am not advocating that we allow prophecies which contain inaccuracies to be given without any feedback to the person concerned, but I am using this example to underscore that prophecy is more than simply a communication of various facts. Prophecy has a 'spirit', a 'flow' or a 'direction' to it, and it is this spirit which we must initially weigh. Once a prophecy has been given and we have discerned that the spirit of the word lines up with the heart of our Father, we can then move on to look at the details of what has been shared.

So here we have a vital principle which will help us in weighing prophecy. Alongside asking how it lines up with Scripture, we would ask: How does it 'witness' with our own spirits? We do of course need to acknowledge that we will have a tendency to reject a word if it does not line up with our own desires. This is where there is safety and objectivity in a number of more mature believers bringing their discernment to bear on such prophecies. The converse is also true, where we might be prone readily to accept a word which is simply confirming our own desires.

If a prophecy for an individual or a church contains significant content or direction, I would recommend that it be recorded—perhaps on tape at first, but eventually in writing—as this will help when we come to weigh it in more detail. A word which is recorded is then accessible for the comment of other mature people. Allowing mature Christians whom we trust to make their objective comments on what has been spoken is another important principle in the weighing of prophecy.

As we weigh prophecy it is good to remember that it will not contain every detail (1 Cor 13:8). There will always be gaps in what is communicated; that way we do not lose the need to seek God for ourselves. Prophecy was never intended to replace our need of a first-hand relationship with God. In fact when true prophecy is received it should lead us to seek the face of God even more than before.

Alongside weighing prophecy we will also need to apply a measure of interpretation to the word, particularly if it contains significant content and direction. A critical area for interpretation is the timing of the fulfilment of the words spoken. A further complication occurs when some of the events spoken of might well be future but the language used is present tense. This can occur at times because God does not relate to the future in the same way that we do. God wants us to know that the future is as certain as the present when his word is embraced and responded to with faith.

Many times prophecy is given to prepare us for the future (Amos 3:7) so that we can begin to pray in line with the revealed will of God. This was how Paul instructed Timothy to respond to the prophecies that had been given over him. He encouraged Timothy to fight his own battles in line with the prophecies which he had received (1 Tim 1:18). If prophecy speaks of future events our role is to pray that those words are fulfilled in line with God's word.

The fulfilment of prophecy is not automatic. Virtually all prophecy contains conditions—either explicit or implicit. So, for example, God's word to Israel was conditional and many died in the wilderness not experiencing the fulfilment of that promise because they had not actively mixed God's word with faith (Heb 4:2).

Having weighed a prophecy in spirit we might still need to seek God for wisdom and understanding concerning the fulfilment of that word. We will often need further insight to help us interpret the original word and also to find out what is required of us in order to see it fulfilled. So it will be vital for us to engage in prayer in order to see God's word fulfilled. Often through this process God will do a work in us which will help to prepare us for the prophecy's fulfilment.

We see then that when it comes to weighing prophecy both the test of Scripture and the accuracy of the word are important, but these two alone are not sufficient guidelines. In the final analysis prophecy is weighed from our spirits and so highlights the need for us all to grow in maturity and spiritual wisdom. If currently there is a genuine recovery of the gift of prophecy there is also a need for genuine spiritual maturity to go alongside it. If not, we might well repeat the errors of the past.

Having looked at some aspects of weighing prophecy it is now appropriate to look at the development of prophetic ministry. I am convinced that God is not only restoring prophecy but he is also releasing mature prophetic ministries into the church. The emergence of such ministries is vital if the church is to grow to maturity. However, it is also vital that we learn how to respond to them and the message they bring.

'And some to be prophets' (Eph 4:11)

It would appear that Paul accepted the possibility of all believers prophesying (1 Cor 14:1, 31), but considered that the prophetic 'office' was not open to all (Eph 4:11; 1 Cor 12:29). We can therefore make a distinction between someone with a prophetic ministry and someone who simply moves in the gift of prophecy. In his letter to the Ephesians Paul describes prophets as having a foundational role in churches alongside those with an apostolic gift (Eph 2:20). The prophets of the Old Testament were originally called 'seers' (1 Sam 9:9)—not because they all had amazing three-dimensional visions, but because they were 'seeing' something in the spiritual realm. They were men and women of revelation. This ability to 'see' characterises the ministry of those called to be prophets. In the church context they bring revelation regarding the will and purpose of God at a given time. Such revelation is foundational to a church and many times it will be necessary for those with apostolic gifting to help implement the prophetic revelation. If expertise in building a church is one of the hallmarks of those with apostolic gifting (1 Cor 3:10), it is easy to see why the combination of the apostle and prophet is so effective.

In Ephesians 3:7–13 Paul states that the Ascended Christ gives gifts to individuals in order that the church might reach a place of maturity. If God is indeed maturing his church then we can expect to find an increasing number of prophets emerging in our churches. We might also expect some false prophets to appear and therefore it is essential for there to be teaching concerning the whole prophetic sphere. Without such teaching there will be much confusion as many react to the increase of prophetic ministry.

Although prophets may receive help and training through many human sources and channels, a true prophet is someone who has been appointed by God and his or her primary training will be from him. This is seen clearly in the case of Hosea who understood the broken heart of God over his people, not simply through some cerebral understanding, but through the pain of his own marriage. His experience paralleled that of his God. The true prophet's message is more than the simple communication of facts which are true. Words may well be involved in explaining the heart of God, but the message will have been worked out in the prophet's life beforehand. Jesus seemed to indicate that Abel was in fact the first prophet—as far as we know Abel did not prophesy verbally, but his death spoke prophetically because his life was prophetic (Lk 11:50–51). In Amos we read that God shows his prophets what he is going to do. Many times this is not simply objective revelation, but it is understood through the subjective experience and burden placed upon a person's life.

In the Book of Revelation John was told to prophesy, but before he could do so he had to eat the word of God (Rev 10:9–11). As John ate God's revelation he found that it became sour in his stomach. He did not experience a great thrill at receiving God's revelation—rather it burdened him. To one degree or another all prophets who have been appointed by God will carry a burden from God as they seek to be faithful to the God they represent and serve.

A prophet's reward is to know that they are approved by God as they seek to help the church fulfil its destiny. It is clear that there should be a great dependence on God in the life and ministry of a prophet. However, it needs to be emphasised that prophets are not to separate themselves from the rest of the body of Christ. We all need relationships, and the context in which a prophet operates is the church, the family of God. The prophet cannot adopt some mystical aura which keeps people at a distance. There might well be seasons when someone with prophetic ministry will need to withdraw in order to seek God, but this should never be in order to prevent people gaining access to his or her life. We all need to be in submission to the body, and prophets are certainly no exception—the very nature of their ministry demands otherwise.

Someone who prophesies will strengthen, encourage and comfort the church (1 Cor 14:3). Although prophets will not contradict this principle, they will often go beyond it. Jeremiah was called to destroy and to build (Jer 1:10), and prophets will sometimes need to speak strong corrective words as well as those which confirm. When corrective words are needed the underlying motivation will be that of protecting the church. Correction and direction which come through the ministry of a prophet will, like all words which are claimed to come from God, need weighing.

Prophets are necessary for the church to become a mature bride for Christ and it is important that the leadership of churches open their doors to those with proven prophetic ministry. Those who claim to have such a ministry need to be seen to function within the normal parameters of the Christian life. The church needs the prophetic ministry and prophets need to be in submission to those in leadership.

In closing, I want to make certain requests: first, that we open our churches to prophetic ministry; secondly, that we look to encourage and develop those with the prophetic calling on their lives; and thirdly, that we do not allow prophets whose motivation is self-promotion and whose lives are unteachable to develop unchecked.

I believe that if we ignore the above requests then we will live to regret it. This is our hour of opportunity and the prophetic ministry alongside all the other ministries will prove to be invaluable to us.

supply of sweet, soft water would be available. The parchment's final instructions were to refill the container for the next traveller's use.

The man faced a dilemma: he was dying of thirst and he had found water; not much, of course—maybe not even enough to save his life—but it seemed the height of folly to pour it away down the base of the pump. On the other hand, if the note was accurate, by pouring out the small quantity of water, he would then have all he wanted. What should he do?*

Failing to invest

The tragic record of history is this: the church has consistently drunk the water out of the glass and failed to pour it out and thus make available an unlimited supply. The church has failed to invest in its present, let alone its future. One only has to examine the history of the church to see time after time movements of God dramatically affecting a generation, but that generation failing to invest in the next generation. Within a matter of a few years, the blessing of God has been diluted to a mere shadow of its former glory, leaving ritual and legalism without life or vitality.

Many are sensing that we stand at such a point in history. We stand with the glass of water in one hand and the parchment in the other. Are we to receive immediate satisfaction by drinking from the water, or are we to take the risk and face the possibility that the writer of the parchment was a liar and we could be facing a short, sharp death?

We are also facing the possibility that the investment of a small amount of water would release much more which would quench the needs of thousands, even millions, and indeed perhaps herald the coming of the end of this age.

---

* This parable is adapted from one given by Jim Carpenter in *Discipleship Journal*

Change is in the air

In whatever denomination or stream we find ourselves, there is a growing awareness that change is in the air. We don't quite know what God has in mind, but we do know that things aren't going to stay the same. The challenge for those of us in what have been described as the 'New Churches' is: Are we going to hear the next thing that God is asking of us? And if we are, are we willing to invest all that God has done with us over the last few years into all that God has in mind for the future?

You will recall the parable of the ten virgins, told by Jesus and recorded in Matthew 25:1ff. The foolish virgins were the unprepared ones. They knew the bridegroom was coming—they were dressed ready for the feast, they had their lamps—but they had failed to prepare and they didn't have the spare oil. I would like us to consider briefly four areas of investment which the church will disregard at its peril as it prepares for the twenty-first century.

Investing in expansion

Historically, our immediate roots in the New Churches are to be found in the charismatic movement and the community/restoration movement. These movements, particularly at grass-roots level, have often been characterised by introversion and pastorally dominated structures. A major emphasis over the last two decades has been the building of church, the establishing of relationships, the release of the gifts of the Holy Spirit and discipleship. Now we must not decry all that has been going on, clearly under the direction of God's Holy Spirit, over these last ten to twenty years. Indeed, it has obviously been God's timing and his emphasis to his church. But let us also recognise that it is not the whole story.

God has established his church to be the agent of his kingdom. The kingdom of God is fundamentally expansionist and involves a taking of territory. Satan, the god of this world (2 Cor 4:4), has lied, cheated, robbed and deceived his way into areas of control and influence in this world. Salvation history as recorded through the pages of the Bible (both Old and New Testament) sees God's rescue plan for mankind. The Great Commission of Matthew 28 and Mark 16 sees salvation history brought into the arena of the church and leaves us with the mandate of the kingdom—to go into all the world, to make disciples, to baptise and to teach. If we are to be an expression of the church that Jesus is building, we must embrace this expansionist mandate—a mandate which will not have been fulfilled until 'this gospel of the kingdom will be preached in the whole world as a testimony to all nations, and then the end will come' (Mt 24:14).

If we are going to invest in expansion, then there are structural implications for the churches in which we are involved. James Engels says this: 'You can have all the harvest equipment, but without the blades you are useless.' I look around the church in this country and am at times gripped with real fear. We can spend a lot of time building our barns, making sure the mill is working, getting the oven ready and indeed even working hard at maintaining the harvesters. But if the harvesters have no blades, we are wasting our time. Jesus instructed his disciples to pray that the Lord of the harvest would send forth labourers into his harvest. The words 'send forth' come from the same root used by Jesus to describe driving out a demon. We should also notice that Jesus never instructed his disciples to pray regarding the fields. He looked out at the fields and said they were ripe, ready for harvest, but the problem was always to do with how the harvest was to be brought in.

We need to sense afresh the urgency expressed in the prayer of Jesus, 'Drive out workers to collect the harvest.' Not 'to maintain the harvesters', not 'to build the barns', not 'to bake the bread' but 'to collect the harvest'. We can spend so much time and energy 'building church' when Jesus never instructed us to do it. Indeed, he promised us that he would build the church.

I have recently begun to challenge leaders to research the percentage of their own church's time and money which is spent on maintenance, keeping the church happy, changing the saints' nappies, and the percentage spent on expansion. The results of such research can often be quite shocking.

Investment in expansion also raises questions with regard to the basic structuring of our church. In many churches the house group has become the central focal point for fellowship and care, but many are now facing the grave danger of pastoring people into the ground. Indeed, much of what has been termed 'pastoring' has actually been the maintaining of immaturity in the church, rescuing members of the house group from the next crisis to befall them.

Investing in expansion means facing some difficult decisions. Some churches are already tackling the sacred cow of the house group; establishing functioning teams with expansionist mandates; asking pastors to pastor, but without a weekly house-group meeting, and establishing specialist care groups for those who really need it, such as new Christians and young people. At the same time, they are freeing the mature to pursue their calling in God, to get to know their neighbours, workmates, family and friends without the continual battle of the demands of the church diary. The church diary can so easily separate us from the very people the church is desiring to reach.

Investment in expansion means we need to be considering the make-up of our eldership/leadership teams. Historically, these have been dominated by the more pastorally orientated ministries. This has brought certain strengths but also certain weaknesses. On the strength side, it has resulted in stability, continuity and care. But on the weakness side, it has resulted in a resistance to change, a cautious approach to all issues, a lack of vision and a non-expansionist view of the church. If we are to invest in expansion, we need to be considering widening our leadership teams to include those with prophetic and evangelistic orientations.

How we are to deal with the challenge of an expansionist investment will vary from one situation to the next, but Scripture is quite clear that if God is developing new wine, it is dangerous for us to be sticking to old wineskins.

Investing in the young

The fact is, we are all getting older; the problem is, we don't realise it. When I was nineteen years of age, I was leading a coffee-bar ministry in the centre of Copenhagen, preaching in churches around Denmark and about to lead an international team of evangelists on a summer mission. How many of the young people in your church will get those kinds of opportunities?

The Apostle Paul included the youthful Timothy in his apostolic team and was then forced to warn him in 1 Timothy 4:12, 'Don't let anyone look down on you because you are young.' While probably still in his early twenties, he was Paul's representative establishing churches and appointing elders. As I travel around many of our churches (and I am talking about New Churches, not just established denominational churches), I fear I am seeing the beginning of a 'back row'. If you don't know what a back row is, let me tell you. Most evangelical churches have one. The back row is made up of young people who belong to the youth group. The problem is this: you can't go to the youth group unless you go to the evening meeting. But you don't want to go to the evening meeting. And so you go, not wanting to be there and making sure everybody else knows it. If we are going to see what God has invested in us passed on to the next generation, we have a crucial role in winning our young people.

Statisticians tell us that the optimum age for becoming a Christian is fourteen years nine months. Investing in youth evangelism is a sound investment. Close on 70% of the church I belong to became Christians in their teenage years. We need to win our young people and then get them to win their friends. Having won their friends we need to turn them into leaders. For God's sake, let us not turn them into pew fodder: nice middle-class yuppies with nice careers, nice cars, nice homes, but often useless for the kingdom of God.

Our young people need to be sensing that they own what we are doing, and that they are being prepared to take it on for themselves. Unless we are prepared to invest in our young people, we will have nobody to hand it on to. I sometimes wonder, if there was a young Gerald Coates, Roger Forster, Lynn Green or Jackie Pullinger growing up in our church, would we develop them, train them and encourage them, or would they have to leave us in order to be who God has called them to be?

Our young people need opportunities to lead, to influence, to speak. They need challenges, they need taking seriously and they need training.

There is a cost to be paid if we are going to invest in our young people. It is going to cost us time, it is going to cost us effort and we will need to take a few risks. They will let us down, they won't do it quite as we wanted it done—but they might just pick up the mantle and do it better than ever we could.

Investing in training

If we are going to see the move of God in this country that many of us are looking for, training becomes crucial. We were recently faced with this issue in my home church as we began to contemplate church planting. We suddenly began to realise that we had lots of good solid pastors, worship leaders and a few keen on the children's work, but we didn't have many we felt could be released to lead a team in planting a church. Indeed, as we began to look at the situation we realised that although we might carry many reservations regarding the functioning of Bible schools, our three full-time workers were at the time all Bible school trained. As a result of these deliberations we are now running discipleship groups in public ministry and leadership. The groups were started by each member of the group being challenged by three questions. First, what are your aspirations? Secondly, where are you at present? Thirdly, how do you see yourself getting from where you are to where you want to be?

Gerald Coates has said, 'The only difference between aspiration and achievement is development.' Development is all about training. Jesus had a training programme for his disciples and so should we. If we aren't going to send people off to Bible school, then the New Churches are going to have to come to terms with how they are going to train their people in church planting, as mission workers and public ministries.

Each church needs its own strategy for the training and

development of its people. Training might be 'in-house', with specialist ministries brought in to supplement the resources of the church. Or it might be 'out-house', sending individuals in the church on conferences, study courses or training teams. The training course might involve the preparation of Bible studies, reading specific books, listening to particular tapes, preparing short talks, leading meetings. Whenever you get people to do something, make sure you give them feedback on how well they did and how they could improve. Jesus gave it to his disciples —it's the only way people learn.

Let us also make sure we are not simply spewing out a vast body of knowledge but are imparting skills which can be used for life. I recently observed my young son Jake climbing a low wall. Halfway up the wall he got stuck. His immediate response was to cry out, 'Mummy! Mummy! Get me down!' Mummy turns up on the scene, but rather than lifting Jake from the wall, she teaches him how to descend a step at a time. Two minutes later, Jake climbs a similar low wall, getting stuck in a similar position. He assesses the situation and realises that he has the skills to descend— which he does without the necessity of any parental intervention. We can so often spend our lives lifting people off walls rather than teaching them how to climb down themselves and thus imparting a skill which could be used time and time again.

Investing in opportunities

Training without opportunities will create nothing but frustration. But opportunities linked with training will provide a hunger for further training. In Pioneer's TIE (Training In Evangelism) Teams we are always looking to link training with action. The problem faced in many of our churches is that many of our people genuinely feel that all the jobs are taken. Furthermore, those of us doing the jobs—whether it is leading a team, leading a group, counselling, administrating or public ministry—are getting better and better at them because we have the opportunities to do them. We thus find that the gap gets wider and wider between those of us who are doing the jobs and those who aren't and, of course, the standards get higher and higher.

I understand Billy Graham tells the story of his first evangelistic message. He prepared three sermons so that he might be sensitive to what God wanted to say on that particular evening. The problem Billy Graham faced was that he had preached all three sermons in the first ten minutes! If we are going to develop people, we need to be providing them with opportunities to be preaching three sermons in ten minutes. Opportunities for them to learn, to make mistakes, to push back fear, to develop faith, to take risks and to do things differently.

We also need to face the fact that many church leaders suffer from a very serious disease which is called 'people blindness'. I was recently talking to the leader of a medium-sized church. We were talking through his evangelism strategy. The leader told me. 'The problem is, we don't have the right person to head it up. If only we had, I'd send them on TIE Teams, see them trained and perhaps get them out full time.' A friend of mine was standing close to this conversation. He had been doing some evangelism training in that particular church and he interrupted us. 'Have you thought about . . . ?' he asked.

'Oh no!' the leader replied in genuine surprise. 'I'd not thought of him.'

'And what about . . . ?'

'No, I'd not thought about him.'

And so it was that three names were mentioned, none of whom the leader had seriously considered, but all of whom were potential candidates for the job he was considering. The leader was convinced he had nobody, but in fact he had three potential evangelism leaders sitting in his congregation.

The problem is that leaders are often blind. They have known people since they were children, but they could now be grown-up. They have counselled them in their problems, but maybe they are through them now. I encourage leadership groups to work through their address list and look with fresh eyes at the people they have, asking the Holy Spirit to enlighten them as to where they are now. I am convinced that in many churches around the country we have locked-up resources (people) whom God wants to see released.

As we are considering opportunities, we need also to recognise that some people are never going to be fully developed with just local opportunities. We need to be prepared to break out of our local church mentality and recognise that we are part of a far larger thing—God's church internationally. God is calling people to work overseas, eg, working short term or long term in evangelism, education, medicine, carpentry, printing, technical service. The list is as endless as the opportunities. We need to recognise God calling and provide strategy, training and support towards these ends.

Investing is important

While some might wish to question some of my conclusions, I am hoping that most would agree with the heart of what has been shared. I wish to conclude by addressing the question, 'What would stop us from investing?'

The fact of the matter is this—we're not going to invest in the future unless we see that investing is important; and we're not going to invest unless we are sure there is going to be some hope of a return.

We're not going to invest if we are fearful of change. Change brings tensions and conflicts, but we have to face the fact that if God is for change, we are either running with him or we are running against him. Christendom is littered with monuments to what God once said. But they are monuments because they failed to respond to what God said next. We won't invest if we are fearful of rocking the boat, of upsetting people, of risking making mistakes, of changing the status quo. But whose boat is it anyway? Whose church is it? Whose people are we leading, caring for and training?

We won't invest if we live continually with the question, 'How will this affect me, my ministry, my friends, my status?' Leaders have more to lose than most. Are we willing to be overtaken? Are we willing to pass on what God gave to us? Are we willing to take off our crowns and pass them on to another generation? Are we willing to live with a few tensions and conflicts as people learn, mature and make mistakes? God has done that with us—shouldn't we do that for others? Shouldn't we take the risk of pouring the glass of water down the hole in the pump with the hope that, as a result, an unlimited supply of fresh water will become available? Shouldn't we take the risk that through our investment we might see opened what has been locked up in our churches for years and see it released for the glory of God and the expansion of his kingdom?

5
Having a Vision—Making It Happen

Adrian Hawkes

Adrian Hawkes leads a network of churches and ministries entitled 'New Living Ministries' which is a part of the Pioneer work. The main church is based in the famous rock theatre, The Rainbow, on Seven Sisters Road in North London. They are involved in a number of church-planting initiatives in North London and have inroads into the Tamil community and are church planting with them in France, Switzerland and New Zealand. Adrian is married to Pauline and they have three children.

If you take a jam-jar and fill it with fleas (the jumping kind), placing the lid firmly on for your own protection, you should note that the fleas will jump up and down until they bang their heads on the lid. At that point they will reduce the height of their jump to a point just below the rim. Fleas, apparently, don't like bumping their heads. I am told that if you later remove the lid, the fleas will continue to stay in the jar because they are conditioned to believe in a lid.

I have not done this experiment myself, but you are welcome to try it. The point is they are conditioned. Most of us are conditioned by what is around us. It encloses us, it limits us, it controls us. If we understood what a big God we have, we would understand that he has taken the limits off and we can jump out of our jar and we can move on. We can be better and bigger

achievers, and far more. But we have to know that those socio-
logical, cultural, upbringing and educational limits have actually
been removed and now it is up to us to jump out.

Breaking the vicious circle

People come to look at the work that has been achieved in our
church here in North London and often say things like, 'If only I
had . . . then I could. . . .' It is foolish to look at what is and
assume that it has always been, or that everything floated down
from heaven, ready made, just for that pastor, team, leader, music
director or whatever, to take charge of and enjoy the fruits.

In every situation there is always the vicious circle. It goes
something like this. We do not have enough people; if we had the
right money we could get the people; we also lack resources. To
some extent that is often a correct conclusion, but somewhere
those circles must be broken. We have some choices to make, and
the key to those choices is vision—not looking at what is, but at
what could be. Not looking at who you have with you, but at what
they are going to become. Not looking at the money you don't
have, but at knowing how much you need to spend.

It takes vision plus faith to break the circle. You might break it
at the financial point; you might break it at the resources point;
you might well break it at the point of people whom you do have
and know and who are willing to be with you to help.

Most people have what I call tunnel vision: they see what they
want to see. They see what they are conditioned to see, what logic
tells them they should see. The mind fills in the details. Almost
like the fact that the action of the mind prefers to compensate for
the blind spot in the eye, filling in the details from past experiences.
We need to jump out of that mind-set. We need new thinking—
lateral thinking. 'Put on the mind of Christ,' the Bible says. Dream
dreams! Have a vision!

Chickens

Chickens could tell us a lot. A farmer once told me that, as a child,
he used to play a game with farmyard chickens. He would catch

a hen, firmly push its beak to the ground and then, with a finger, draw a line in the farmyard dirt. The hen would watch from the right eye the line being drawn nearer and nearer to its head. When the finger got to the head, he would run the finger firmly across the chicken's head so that it really felt it, and then down the other side of the head. He then continued the line along the dirt, which the hen watched with great suspicion with its left eye. The hen could see a line with the right eye and a line with the left eye, and it surely felt it go across its head. Then he would gently release his hold on the chicken which would stay right there, tied to the floor. It could see the rope with both eyes. The chicken had felt the rope over its head; it knew it was tied down.

Some of us can see what we see, but we see it only with our human eyes. We fail to see with vision that is clear. We can only see the reason why we have not succeeded, the reason why we have been tied down, the reason why we did not get the breaks.

You are not too old. It is not too late to have a dream, to have a vision and to plan the first steps. You will then discover that the things that tied you down were actually illusions, and were only there to limit you in what you need to do for the kingdom.

Elephants

They tell me that the way to train an elephant is very simple. Again, I have not tried it, but will be glad to receive the results of your research. I am told that you find a sturdy tree stump and tie the elephant's leg to it with a strong chain. You then put food for the elephant just out of reach so that as he moves towards it the chain cuts harder into his leg, creating considerable pain. After a few days, the elephant learns that to try and reach the food simply causes tremendous pain and is unachievable. You can then feed the elephant. You can change the chain for a light rope that normally the elephant would snap, but the light rope will now be sufficient to restrain your elephant.

The elephant has been conditioned to believe that moving his leg, if it is tied, would cause him pain. So he has learned to move only in the area where the slack would allow. Conditioned, controlled and tamed, the mighty elephant is now limited. There is one thing, however, that will spoil the training of an elephant. Should you have completed your training and then be unfortunate enough to suffer a fire (one that comes towards your elephant), the fire would enable the elephant to overcome the conditioning, overcome the pain, overcome the fact that he knows he is tied, and he would break loose. The breaking loose would mean that never again could you train him or condition him. You have lost your elephant!

Changing our thinking

It is very obvious that the way God changes people is by changing their thinking. 'As a man thinks, so he is,' says Proverbs 23:7 in effect. 'Be transformed by the renewing of your mind' (Rom 12:2). What we think about ourselves, our situation, our upbringing, our God, is all-important. 'I am unable' means you will not be able to. 'I can' means you will. Paul says, 'I can do everything through him who gives me strength' (Phil 4:13), and he could!

The fire changes the elephant and makes him free once again. The fire of the Holy Spirit should burn into our minds and set us free. Maybe some of us speak in tongues, but we somehow need the fire of the Holy Spirit to burn up the old negatives—the disillusionment, conditioning, upbringing, old hurts, laziness, world-liness, wrong conceptions of God—and free us to be visionaries who will take action and change the world. This is how it happened in the Bible. I am not trying out a new doctrine.

Danny Moe, a Canadian friend of mine, takes seminars for sales representatives for some very large companies. He told me once that fewer than 1% of all groups (and he does seminars for secular as well as Christian organisations) have any goals, plan or vision of where they are going or what they plan to be or do. A pastor of a church in North London spoke to me at a Ministers' Fraternal. When I asked him what his goals and aims were, his answer was, 'I am just waiting to be led. I do not plan anything. I just want to see what God does.' That sort of nonsense showed in the life, or rather non-life, of his church!

I am sure that God is still willing to speak with us, guide us and redirect us, but there is a broad-based plan in Scripture that offers scope for us to change the situation. God is with us to do just that.

How do we get started?

How do we change if we are visionless at the moment? Where do you get dreams from?

I believe the first place we ought to go is to the word of God in order to gain understanding of who God is and what he is able to do. Fill your mind with it. Fill your mind with the fact that he is a mighty God, a God of miracles, a God of power, God who is love. Know that he is with you, for you, plans for your success, is just waiting to be involved with your work, and for you to be involved with his plans.

Secondly, start to dream—not necessarily while you are asleep! Dreams without inhibition, unlimited dreams. Do not limit your dreams by what your qualifications are, or what you don't have, or what you may or may not need, or what resources you lack. Dream as if you have them all.

Thirdly, begin to have a vision of the dreams fulfilled. See it, taste it, walk round it, hear from God, tell him what you see.

Fourthly, set goals—real goals, long-term goals, short-term goals, medium-term goals—and say: 'My goals take me there. My long-term goal is to arrive.' The goals must interlink. It is not usually sensible to go south if your ultimate plan is to end up in the north. Write the goals down. Review them regularly. Life is made up of choices and some things have to be rejected in favour of others. Don't get side-tracked and channelled into the wrong direction from your goal. God is for you, so go for it! Remember that destiny is a matter of choice not circumstance.

Fifthly, and here is where many people get frozen in their tracks (where dreams and visions may die), have a plan of where you are going. You must have bite-size, achievable objectives. To put it another way, the goal must be broken down into small pieces. What will you do tomorrow? These composite parts of your vision must have time limits. They must be measurable. You might miss the time or not quite make the measurement, but if it is not stated, then it is not measurable and you will hit nothing and go nowhere. (Unless of course you are like the farmer who hit a bull's eye every time on his barn door. The only problem was, he painted the targets after he had fired the bullets.)

Sixthly, we need a philosophy of ministry. We need to be reminded at this point that we are kingdom people, children of the heavenly Father. We cannot regard what we do as simply employment, though we may be employed. We cannot see it as just work, though we may have to work very hard.

Ministry

The best way of describing what we do to accomplish the vision, is ministry. That means you and your vision are not only working something out, you are a gift to the church. Not a cheap copy that will break down after a couple of uses, but a real valuable genuine article. What is ministry? Where do we minister? It seems that many definitions of ministry have a very narrow band—preaching, visiting, studying. There are some who would tag other gifts to the church with that, such as teacher or pastor. From my own perspective, it has been a great tragedy that many denominations see the pastoral role as the main ministry and only pay lip service to the other ministries. We need a philosophy of ministry that is broad based, enabling, involving and one that will allow us to be inclusive of the whole church community.

I have tried to work out a philosophy of ministry as follows:

1. To be an enabler—which usually means getting out of the way to let the church work.

2. To have the broadest possible vision. I would see that as the local church being involved in every angle and aspect of human happening—worship, praise, evangelism, education, business, medicine, politics and social concern.

3. To have a vision broad enough to allow me to incorporate other people's vision into my vision making it *our* vision, and

to help them exercise their ministry in the widest possible way.

4. To seek to obey the biblical injunction to pass on to faithful men that which I have learned, that they in turn pass it on (2 Tim 2:2), and to allow that participation across the whole ministry. I do not imagine that I will always be the preacher, teacher or whatever, or that the team around me will always be doing what they are doing. They must be passers-on and developers of others.

5. To seek to have structures that teach the church and then the community at large to bring forth facets of ministry, so that care takes place for the whole church.

6. To seek to be expansionist in every area of church activity. Remember that evil is expansionist and therefore the kingdom needs to be as well.

7. To continually find other people's ministries and develop them. I do not mean that you must adopt my philosophy of ministry, but you do need one. Many do not have one. They are going through the motions of a tradition, or they have a job, or they have never taken the trouble to define what they are about. Think it through, define it and go for it! If you are not planning to hit something, then most likely you won't! This may put some off because of the 'hard work' factor.

Reaction

We had quite a substantial work in North London and God blessed us in many ways. We spent considerable time showing people around the numerous facilities. Most of the people we showed around were church leaders of various ilk. The reaction concerning what God had done usually came in three forms:

(a) Those who regarded me, or the team, or both, as something unique, specially used of God, a one-off. This is not a compliment because we are very ordinary people. Usually visitors said, 'If I had your . . . ' and named some aspect of our church's talents, ministry or plant as if it had fallen down from heaven. It did not. It took battles, disappointments, despondency, misunderstandings, stickability, faith in God and sheer hard work.

(b) The second group, who perhaps were a little more honest, looked around and said, 'Oh, it's great, but it looks like hard work to me. I would not want to cope with so much.' Sadly, that group seemed to be the largest.

(c) The third group, and by far the smallest, looked and said, 'I can see what God has done for you. He can do similar things in my church/town/area. I am going to become the catalyst for change in my sphere of influence.'

I believe in models. I believe in setting trends, in challenging what is. It is only as some do, in God, what has not been done before that others will follow. I don't think it is wrong to want some of the good things God has done for others. They are my chance to know him more, to enter into a deeper relationship and to experience his working. I noticed that Jesus called busy people in the New Testament to follow him. He did not call those who were sitting around doing nothing. I think work can be great fun, especially when it is kingdom work.

8. I do believe leadership must set goals so that visions do not become a one-man show, or just personal vision. Their vision must be something the whole church can see and go for. I often go into other churches and I am told what the vision of the church is. Sadly many times there isn't one. Worse still, people often say to me, 'Tell our pastor what is going on in your fellowship so some of it can go on here.' It is not as simple as that. Many pastors don't want to hear or know! It is possible to have a people-led revolution, but it is usually bloody, hurtful and often does not succeed. Much better if a leadership has vision, translates it into goals and persuades others to own those goals.

Some years ago I came back from a Pastors' School with what I believe was a vision from God, or word from the Lord—a goal. It was to become a church that is an effective visible voice for him in our area of North East London, with at least 3,000 people coming together for celebrations. We have not arrived there yet, but if you had asked people in our fellowship, one year later, 'What is the goal of the church?' 10% would have said, 'A congregation of 3,000.' If you ask that question now, 90% would give you the same answer.

9. You have to start somewhere and the best thing to start with is what you have got. Too many people claim they are going to do 'so and so' when God sends the person with 'such and such' a gift or talent to the church. They will do it when finances are right, or, worse still, when the church is right.

God gives the increase

We need to learn from the two little ones who were late for school. One said, 'Let's stop and pray that the bus will be late.' The other one said, 'No, let's run and pray.' It seems to me that God wants to do a great deal with the little we do have. We need to see and be willing to use the little we have if we want God to move for us.

God's miracles always seem to have a human element in the Bible. Here are three examples to demonstrate what I mean.

(a) 'What have you got?' asked the starving Elijah of the starving widow. 'Nothing,' was the first reply. The second reply was, 'Except some oil and meal.' 'Bake it and give it to God,' was the answer. God gives the increase (see 1 Kings 17:7–16).

(b) 'What have you got?' the man of God asked of the widow who says her children will be sold into slavery. 'Nothing,' was the first reply. The second reply was 'Except a little oil.' 'Go and collect vessels and use your oil,' said Elisha. God gives the increase (see 2 Kings 4:1–7).

(c) 'Feed the people,' Jesus commanded the disciples. 'How?' they asked. 'What have you got?' asked Jesus. 'Nothing,' was the first reply. 'Five loaves and two fishes,' was the second reply. God gives the increase (see Matthew 14:15–21).

I ask many leaders, 'What have you got?' The reply is often that they have nothing. Because my eyes are adjusted to seeing, I go to their churches and see talents of music, witnessing, service and caring, and I long to have them say to God, 'I have these and I give them to you. I will use them. I will start.' Then they will see God give the increase.

Having started—continue. So often we want to give up because it is hard, it is not what we expected, we were misunderstood, it is a pressure, those we trusted have left. But the end is not just

yet. The story is not finished, the climb is not over. Stay with it.
Don't cancel, don't close, don't sell. Invest instead. Don't call it
a day, don't give up. Stay in there and God will give you the
increase. Sow liberally and reap the harvest. There are lots of
great starters, a few good continuers, even fewer finishers. Be one
of the few finishers. Finish what God has called you to do.

10. When you start to go forward, you will need an essential
ingredient—real friends. Friends who will support you. Friends
who will understand you when you are hard to understand.
Friends who are real enough to tell you when you are wrong.
Friends who will be with you when nothing particular is happening. Friends who will stand with you when it seems the sky has
caved in. It will take time to earn such friends. They will need
cultivating. Enjoy meals together, work together, play together.
They will help you and you will help them become all that you
both need to be in the body of Christ.

11. The eleventh thing we need on our way forward is a lack of
neatness. Yes, I did say 'lack'. People who have everything sewn
up have usually stopped church. Those who have everything in
neat tidy committees are not going anywhere. People who want
every 'i' dotted and every 't' crossed before they start out will
probably never leave home. Our Western minds like the tidy
approach, everything in its place. We think structures, and of
course we need structures to make us function, but they don't
always have to be as tidy as we think!

One pastor visiting my church one day said, 'It is so untidy,
more like a circus.'

'I like circuses,' was my reply.

'What is your leadership structure?' some say to me. I know
what it is at the moment, but it is also like a kaleidoscope,
continually changing. The holder is stable but that is all. We
change things around to meet the changing needs and doors of
opportunity. I am very suspicious of neat answers, neat churches.
Long live the ragged edge! Long live anomalies! Long live
exceptions!

12. It is dangerous to become too introspective. When I was a

little boy my mother allowed me to plant some seeds in the garden. Every day I went along and dug them up to see how they were doing. They didn't do very well! We must not do that with ourselves, nor with that part of the work that God has entrusted to us, but we do need to look back.

We need to look back to what we were before God saved us. We need to look back at what has been done. We need to remember that rough diamond and observe some of the polish now beginning to show. We need to remind ourselves that a life once wasted is now bringing forth fruit. We can go forward. We can conquer. We can be more than conquerors—never mind the toil, never mind the hard work, God is worth it! When you do look back and see those things, it will make you want to rejoice. I believe that God wants us to rejoice in him. Be glad in the Lord, even if there is nothing else to be glad in. But there is, for we can be glad in what we have accomplished.

6

Dealing with Religion

Peter Sanderson

Peter Sanderson is married to Pauline and they have three children. One is married and the other two are still living at home. Peter leads the Surbiton Community Church numbering over 250 and has edited the Pioneer magazine for the last ten years.

Jesus was not religious. In fact he was continually in conflict with the religious leaders of his day. It was the ordinary man in the street who followed him about, happily listening to what he had to say. Jesus was a man of the people. He dressed as they did, he ate and drank as they did, he lived as they did. His words, though not always easily understood, had an authority and impact that contrasted sharply with the religious double-talk of the scribes and Pharisees.

Like Son, like Father

The human Jesus was the exact representation of his Father (Heb 1:3). He enjoyed a perfect relationship with God, revealing the Father's heart in all he said and did. God is not religious—no matter what men might think! Indeed, one Old Testament writer expressed this truth in direct, no-nonsense language when he described God's response to Israel's religiosity: 'I hate your show and pretence—your hypocrisy of "honouring" me with your religious feasts and solemn assemblies . . . Away with your hymns of praise—they are mere noise to my ears. I will not listen to your music, no matter how lovely it is' (Amos 5:21–23, The Living Bible).

God hates religion! Could it be that he still feels the same about some of the activity that goes on, in his name, in the church today?

A correct biblical pattern?

Jesus was not afraid to challenge the teaching of the scribes and Pharisees, accusing them of breaking God's commandments for the sake of their handed-down traditions (Mt 15:3). It is so easy to allow past ways of doing things to become binding upon present and future generations—as if there were only one 'proper' way! In the end people find themselves defending tradition at the expense of both Scripture and the Holy Spirit. If there is a correct biblical way to run the church and establish the kingdom—one that overrides all the problems of cultural behaviour, poverty and wealth, political oppression and doctrinal difference—how is it, after nearly 2,000 years of Christianity, that no one has yet discovered it? The answer is obvious. There is no correct biblical pattern to discover. It just does not exist.

The heart of the matter

Jesus was also willing to identify himself with the prophets of old. He quoted back to the religious leaders the scriptures they knew so well: 'This people . . . honors Me with their lips, but their heart is far away from Me. But in vain do they worship Me, teaching as doctrines the precepts of men' (Mt 15:8–9; cf Is 29:13, NASB).

Isaiah's words are a devastating attack on the humbug of religion. They reveal the mind of God and are as relevant today as when Jesus quoted them. Talk is easy, words are cheap, but the real issues lie within. So much of present-day Christianity is unreal. For many it has become just a matter of going through the motions. Words, actions and attitudes are all saying different things. The voice of the Holy Spirit is drowned by the cacophony of man's plans, programmes, methods, traditions and concepts. Is it any wonder that those outside the church refuse to take it seriously?

Smokescreen

The writers of the early church continued this battle with religion. Paul had to warn believers in Rome, Colosse and Galatia about the dangers of religious narrow-mindedness and legalistic attitudes. The ever-down-to-earth James reminded his readers that just 'listening' was not enough—there had to be some 'doing' as well! While Jesus' best friend, John, wrote that just talking about loving people was not enough—it should actually be demonstrated by putting it into practice.

Yet despite the strength and clarity of such biblical teaching, the church has largely ignored these areas and consequently lost its way. It has declined into an organised institution that is rejected or ignored by the vast majority of ordinary people. Many hold the church to be irrelevant and unnecessary. All they see is a religious smokescreen.

Will the real Jesus please stand up?

Evangelicals in desperation may cry, 'Don't look at the church, look at Jesus!' But in what direction should people look? Jesus has been lost behind this very smokescreen of abstract theology, empty ritual, boring worship, false unity and out-of-date language. Some may 'find' him in a rainbow or a glorious sunset, but in the very place where he ought to be seen—in his church—he is obscured from view by the swirling mists of religious behaviour and meaningless words. No wonder God hates religion!

All that remains is a distorted caricature of the greatest man who ever lived. His teaching, lifestyle and actions have been shot through with historical sentimentality, humanistic concepts, evangelical narrowness and super-spiritual unreality.

For centuries Jesus has been depicted in works of art as either a defenceless babe in his mother's arms or as a weak, effeminate man, hanging on a cross in bloody death. In more recent times churchmen have sought to update this image by turning him into an uncertain Messiah who somehow combined the roles of doctor, psychiatrist and social worker. Alongside this, Evangelicals have consistently portrayed a 'meek and mild', abstinent, unemotional Jesus who lived and acted by the book. With the emergence of the so-called 'charismatic movement' yet another picture has appeared—a Jesus who never seemed to stop praying, healing, witnessing and casting out demons—a sort of New Testament cross between Tarzan and Superman.

These concepts have far-reaching implications. What Christians think and understand about Jesus will usually affect the way they live and act. The one who declared that he was 'the way and the truth and the life' (Jn 14:6) has been devalued in the thinking of many. The historical Jesus is ineffective, the modern Jesus insecure, the evangelical Jesus boring, and the charismatic Jesus unbelievable. Will the real Jesus please stand up?

Religious, irreligious or non-religious?

Christians tend to fall into one of three categories. Today the lines of demarcation are clearer than ever. First of all there are those who are *religious*. The word 'religion' is defined as 'a belief in some higher power', 'rites of worship' and a 'system of belief'. There is nothing wrong with the word. It is what it has come to mean that is the problem.

Religion majors in externals, what people do being more important than what they are. Believers become bound up in the legalistic practices of keeping rules and regulations to maintain their Christianity. Sacred cows are a product of religious concepts. These are unchangable standards that have more to do with satisfying the demands of other Christians than with seeking to please God.

Unreality and deception are further symptoms of a religious

mentality. Openness and confession become obscured as people begin to do the right things for the wrong reasons. Looking right becomes more important than doing right. Religion can lead to a superstitious approach towards Bible reading, prayer, quiet times, church meetings and holy days. In turn these things become more important than areas such as family relationships, forgiveness and integrity.

Secondly, there are those who are *irreligious*. They are not to be confused with the anti-religious humanists or communists who want to see all aspects of Christianity removed from society. Irreligious people are those who deliberately flout biblical principles to prove how 'free' they are. They seek to shock and offend other Christians by their actions. While it is sometimes necessary to challenge and confront those who are apathetic, deceived or in error, it is never acceptable to be rude!

Despite professing to be subject to no man but God alone, and often claiming to have been led or told by the Lord to do many things, the truth is somewhat different. In reality they are living under no authority, pleasing themselves rather than pleasing God. Such a rebellious attitude is as abhorrent to God as the empty façade of religion.

Finally, the third category consists of those who are *non-religious*. These are people seeking to live in the reality and openness of the Spirit and under the authority of God. Motivated by delight rather than duty, they enjoy God, life and the world without compromise, guilt or fear. Their desire is to communicate the good news about Jesus to a godless society by speaking in everyday language and acting in normal ways. They want to be distinctive by what they do rather than by what they don't do!

This is not just idealistic talk and exciting theory. It is reality— a reality that growing numbers of believers are experiencing. It's not so difficult to live out a non-religious Christianity, but there are certain danger areas that need to be carefully watched.

The end result of a Christianity infected with the poison of religious concepts and attitudes is visibly demonstrated in the present state of the church. But spotting ways in which religion exerts its influence is not always easy—no one would catch a cold if they could *see* the germs floating about! There are, however, certain tell-tale danger signs that we need to look out for. . . .

Twentieth-century Pharisees

In New Testament times the Pharisees were well known for certain characteristics: a firm belief in Scripture, orthodox doctrines, separated lives, impeccable public conduct and zealous evangelism. Dressed in special religious clothes and corrupted by their own sense of power, they became totally alienated from the ordinary people they were supposed to represent. Their approach was hardline and unyielding.

They came into immediate conflict with Jesus. His following and authority clearly irritated the Pharisees and his teachings challenged their religious practices. Jesus reserved some of his sharpest rhetoric for them. He continually exposed their hypocrisy, self-righteousness and pride, once calling them a 'brood of vipers' (Mt 3:7). Jesus' longest and most scathing rebuke is found in Matthew 23. In this passage he highlighted their double standards in not practising what they preached, their love of titles and public recognition and the way their attitudes were dominated by finance. Jesus condemned their persecution of those who dared to disagree with them and their arguing over minor matters while ignoring the more important issues of justice, mercy and faithfulness.

Times have not changed. It's only the clothes that are different. Today modern Pharisees inhabit the church, spreading their attitudes and ideas everywhere. There are many who say one thing but do another, many who are influenced by those who hold the purse strings, many who waste their time on second-rate issues and many who seek to drive out those who think or act differently from themselves. This pharisaical spirit will bring legalism and condemnation and will deny the Holy Spirit his rightful place in the church.

Fundamentalism

The dictionary states that 'fundamental' means 'the basis or foundation, the starting point, important, essential'. This is the exact opposite of the effect fundamentalist teaching has sometimes had upon the church! The Jewish temple and synagogues may have been home to the Pharisees in Jesus' time, but in this twentieth century the modern Pharisee can be very much at home in some fundamentalist churches. The old joke about fundamentalism being 'not much fun, very mental and full of "isms"' has lost its humour. The issues are far too serious to be laughed at. Fundamentalism can be so occupied with teaching its followers *what* to think that it forgets to teach them *how* to think.

An example of this is seen in an American fundamentalist magazine. A letter was received from a born-again, Bible-believing lady who had an unconverted husband. She was seeking to live in total submission to her husband, but had encountered a major problem. Her husband wanted her to have sex with potential business clients to help him land some profitable contracts. The lady was in a dilemma. How was she to obey God by being submissive to her husband without at the same time disobeying God by committing adultery? She wrote to the magazine for an answer.

The magazine responded with a clear and passionate reply. It was explained to the lady that, in this case, she should disobey her husband in order to obey the higher charge of God.

This was obviously the right answer, but why did the lady have to write to the magazine in the first place? Why did she feel constrained to write to some impersonal column-writer for help? That her relationship with her husband was not all it should be is obvious from the predicament she found herself in. But it is also a sad reflection upon her relationship with her local church that she did not feel she could approach her church leaders or other Christian friends for advice. It is a cause for real concern that she should be married to such a perverted man, but it is almost unbelievable that the influence of fundamentalist teaching had been so profound that she had lost the ability to think clearly for herself. Fundamentalism is often concerned with its stance in relation to the truth rather than to people. Although the answer was correct, it did not get to the root of the problem. The lady and her husband needed help, not just a terse theological response!

Narrow-minded, inflexible teaching produces narrow-minded, inflexible thinking. Everything is seen in black and white. And this kind of teaching still dominates large areas of the church. Fundamentalism tends to make the gospel irrelevant. The story is told of a burglar who broke into a jewellery store but didn't steal anything—he simply rearranged the price tags! This is often what fundamentalism does. It puts high price tags on issues of secondary value and cheapens the things that really do matter.

Living under law

The biblical position is quite clear: Christians are no longer subject to the law . . 'For sin shall not be your master, because you are not under law, but under grace' (Rom 6:14) . . . not the 'law of the land' (they *are* subject to that), but the written commandments given by God to Moses which had been extended to include various Jewish traditions. This issue is at the very heart of the gospel message—grace (something not earned nor deserved) instead of law. It is a theme that runs through book after book in the New Testament. Yet today millions of believers worldwide are trying to work out their Christian experience under law. When this happened in Paul's day he became angry and actually warned the believers at Galatia that they had been bewitched by a spell of deception (Gal 3:1). Christians should get angry today! Living under law robs them of true liberty—it turns Christianity into a form of rule-keeping and presents a totally false image to those outside the church.

But why does this happen? Paul's words to the Galatian church offer one clue—deception! The devil is keen to rob Christians of their freedom and put them back into a bondage that minimises their effectiveness and distorts their message. Another reason Christians live under law is because *initially* it makes things look better. Sometimes the grace of God seems to take a long time to make external changes! Under law, life becomes more orderly and problems are kept under tight control. The religious instinct that is within each of us raises its ugly head. Law enables man to imagine that he can do things to satisfy God's demands when in fact he is doing things to satisfy himself.

Law will never create life. It can never remove sin, bring peace, build relationships or change lives. Only the grace of God can do that. Law demands full restitution for wrong—grace speaks of love, mercy and forgiveness. Law invokes curses and death—grace bestows blessings and life. Law demands obedience—grace motivates obedience. Law tells man what he should do for God— grace tells man what God has done for him. Law demands holiness and righteousness and any change it produces is purely external— grace cultivates inner attitudes.

Under grace, commandments become promises. Even in the Old Testament some writers could foresee this. Prophets like Jeremiah and Ezekiel spoke about a new covenant and a new spirit. Instead of commandments written upon stone, God would put his law within the hearts of his people.

'Behold, days are coming,' declares the Lord, 'when I will make a new covenant with the house of Israel and with the house of Judah, not like the covenant which I made with their fathers in the day I took them by the hand to bring them out of the land of Egypt, My covenant which they broke, although I was a husband to them,' says the Lord. 'But this is the covenant which I will make with the house of Israel after those days,' says the Lord. 'I will put My law within them, and on their heart I will write it; and I will be their God, and they shall be My people' (Jer 31:31–33, NASB).

And I shall give them one heart, and shall put a new spirit within them. And I shall take the heart of stone . . . and give them a heart of flesh, that they may walk in My statutes and keep My ordinances, and do them. Then they will be My people, and I shall be their God (Ezek 11:19–20, NASB).

The gospel of grace is self-productive and self-defensive. It requires no human schemes or psychological ploys to make it work. It needs no shelter from attack—no satanic force can destroy its effect.

But does this really work today? Can it transform Christianity from a rule-keeping, narrow-minded religious slog into a Spirit-led, life-changing relationship with God? The answer is yes! This is because it no longer depends on man—it depends on Jesus. The death sentence has been passed on man's failure to keep the law in its entirety, and Jesus has paid that penalty in full. In Christ *all* man's obligations are met. Man is now set free to enjoy a new relationship with God. Not on the basis of law-keeping, but on the basis that Jesus will do for people what they have failed to do for themselves. The Law-Giver is also the Law-Keeper and he has taken up residence within the lives of his people. He keeps the law for them! It's all *inside*—a new heart and a new spirit. Law was once like a schoolmaster, but now school is out. Jesus has closed down the school and dismissed the teacher.

Pressure, pretence and condemnation

It's not unusual for preachers to exhort their hearers to pray more, read their Bibles more, witness more and attend more meetings. Many go so far as to contend that social or secular occupations such as watching television, reading newspapers and going to sporting events are worldly and unimportant compared with spiritual activities. Such teaching is usually laced with extreme illustrations, and statistics as to how many people die and go to hell every hour!

People often respond to this in one of three ways. Some seek to pray and witness more—not because they really want to, but because they feel compelled to do so in order to satisfy their own consciences and to live up to the standards of other Christians.

Others try to read, pray and witness more, but never actually succeed. Like many a New Year's resolution, these attempts only last for a few days—it has more to do with perspiration than inspiration! Such people inevitably feel themselves to be failures and are often targets for condemnation and depression.

Then again there are others who hardly read, pray or witness at all but, as a result of the pressure to conform to evangelical standards, they pretend to do so—even to the point of making wildly-exaggerated claims! They fellowship in deception and lies.

This behaviour represents a double tragedy. First, those who are pressurised into 'working for the Lord' in this way are a poor reflection of Jesus and his kingdom. And secondly, the people they come into contact with are often put off by the obvious unreality in the lives they lead.

Dividing the sacred from the secular

Church history teaches many valuable lessons. One that has been largely ignored is the tragedy of the sacred/secular division that resulted from the Reformation. Most Protestants react defensively to any criticism of the Reformation, but not all that happened was good! Reformations tend to breed further reformations. Authority is up for grabs—and any sense of unity is shattered. Some Reformation leaders were as intolerant and narrow-minded as the Roman Catholics they sought to overthrow.

The key to this particular problem is Martin Luther's teaching on the difference between church and state. He drew a distinction between the kingdom of God, in which all true believers were under the authority of Christ, and the kingdom of the world, where all non-Christians were under the jurisdiction of civil law. Although at first sight this may seem acceptable, it has long-term ramifications that are still having negative influences upon the church today.

Luther's 'two kingdoms' theory fostered the idea of the sacred and the secular, whereby the church is responsible for spiritual matters (relationship with God, personal holiness, worship and doctrine) and the worldly authorities look after the material aspects of life (the family, economics, science, literature, politics, commerce and the arts). Pursuits and activities that before the Reformation were under the influence and authority of the church were now regarded as secular. Society became further and further removed from Christian influence. The result was supposed to be a purer, more separated church—but in practice this has not been the case. In the event, these concepts resulted in the increasing failure of society to see God as the Creator of all good. Many believed that God looked after the church and the world looked after itself! This view still prevails today.

This is all totally foreign to the teachings and practices of the early church. They knew no such division. Rather, they recognised the biblical truth that God is actively involved in every aspect of his creation and that his authority holds sway over every facet of society. The idea that God concerns himself exclusively with the church is an erroneous one. Indeed, his purpose is to reveal himself to the world through the church.

The religious spirit that seems to grip so many has found a strong foothold through this dividing of the sacred from the secular. It's time to challenge such thinking. It's time to pull down the man-made barriers. The whole of this world—even the nasty parts—belongs to God. His authority extends from 'shore to shore' right now, not just in some future millennial kingdom! This absolute authority will one day become visible, but not because Christians have retreated into their spiritual ghettos, having developed a so-called Christian culture. Rather, it will come about because they have gone out into the world to extend God's kingdom on earth—free from all legalistic and religious attitudes.

Double standards

By calling certain things secular or worldly, some Christians have drawn up an unwritten list of prohibited activities and places. With the often added pressure of 'What would you do if Jesus came back today and found you?' many a young believer is being straitjacketed into religious attitudes that are a million miles from the heart of God. This has resulted in the emergence of a whole list of double standards in Christian thinking. Nothing is actually put down in black and white, but the implications are strong. A classical music concert is acceptable, but a heavy metal gig is not. Going to the ballet is allowed, but discos, with their pounding beat and flashing lights, are taboo. The cinema (or should it be 'sinema'?) is considered dark and worldly (and who knows what happens in the back row?), but watching films at home on the television is OK.

The list covers many other areas and the ensuing conflict over such issues has caused many Christians, young and old, to be hurt and misunderstood. These hurts are the seeds of division within the church. The generation gap is an invention of the devil and a bitter harvest will be reaped unless attitudes change. It's so easy to be critical and judgemental of others who are allegedly worldly. But isn't it just as worldly to be critical and judgemental of others? These are not attitudes inspired by the Holy Spirit. Beware the hypocrisy of double standards!

Boring lifestyle

This is a difficult area to write about, but the truth has to be faced. It has to be said that many non-Christians are put off Jesus by the boring lifestyle of some believers. Some committed Christians are narrow-minded in their thinking, negative in many of their attitudes (especially towards the world), and dull and dreary in their social life. It's as if God had ceased being creative on the sixth day! Leisure activities, hairstyles, musical taste and fashion are areas that should never be stereotyped. (Why do so many Christians seem to dress in clothes that are a few years behind the latest fashion?) Clones are out! There are no Christian uniforms—people should be free to be themselves, not what others want them to be!

The church should be creative in all its activities, especially in the area of praise and worship. But, sadly, many Christians and many churches are trapped in a colourless, predictable, repetitive way of life. The most daredevil thing some ever do is to eat an 'After Eight' mint at seven-thirty! People are bound up by a religious system and are unable to break free. Miserable sinners have often become miserable saints. It's time for a revival of joy and happiness!

Wearing Christian masks

Because Jesus was secure in his own personal identity and in his relationship with his Father, he was also secure in his relationship with other people. Many Christians today are insecure in all of these areas, often as a result of the legalistic demands and consequent negative effects of religious Christianity. Yet this is not always immediately obvious because such people often hide their insecurities behind various types of Christian mask.

There are *intellectual masks*. Those who wear these masks often talk as if they are right and everyone else is wrong. They tend to argue over minute differences of doctrine and practice, excusing bad attitudes such as disunity, non-involvement and criticism under the pretext of standing for truth! Such people often separate belief from behaviour and only feel secure in meetings that are structured and orderly. This mask covers their inability to relate to people and to the moving of the Holy Spirit. They live in 'safe' areas and do not allow their true feelings to surface. The real tragedy to the wearers of such a mask is that their intellectual approach to Scripture and ministry results in their looking primarily for correct interpretation, sound exegesis and balanced theology. This is not to say that theology and exegesis are unimportant, but they are no substitute for an open mind and the willingness to respond from the heart to what God is saying in the here and now.

There are also *spiritual masks*. These are worn by people who usually say one thing but experience another. They claim to be in victory, but inside they are struggling with uncleanness, bitterness and resentment. In meetings they pray and sing with feeling and enthusiasm, but at home they are often lazy, selfish and miserable. They are often too busy working for the Lord to spend much time with their families. They will even share the bread and wine with people they are not on speaking terms with. Most Christians have experienced these pressures, but a spiritual cover-up hinders the open confession of true feelings, bad attitudes, weaknesses and struggles. This deception produces a pretend Christianity devoid of power and effectiveness.

Then there are *super-spiritual masks*. These are especially popular in charismatic circles. People wearing these masks feel it is unspiritual to enjoy ordinary things. They can't seem to do anything without claiming that the Lord told them to, and they tend to blame the devil for all their problems. They seek special guidance for things the Bible says are obligatory and find spiritual reasons for doing their own thing. This is a mask of unreality. Lives that feed on a constant diet of teaching tapes, Christian paperbacks, visions, dreams, prophecies and high-powered meetings are of little use to anyone. Such people usually find it hard to face up to personal responsibility. They claim by faith healings that clearly have not happened. Such foolishness is a travesty of the gospel and an open invitation to demonic forces.

If the cap fits . . .

Can you recognise yourself somewhere in this chapter? If you are honest, you will. These are the religious pressures that *all* Christians face at one time or another. But don't get defensive. The aim in writing is conviction, not condemnation! When danger is imminent the logical thing to do is to turn around and go the other way. The Bible calls this repentance.

Examine your attitudes and motives before God. Be honest with him and with yourself as to why you do the things you do. Allow the Holy Spirit to direct you and respond to what he says. These danger signs need to be heeded. For the church to be effective in the way God intends, it must become extrovert rather than introvert. As someone has said, 'God can never turn the world upside-down until he has turned the church inside-out.' This will never happen until Christians become more concerned about the world than about the church; more committed to the salvation of the world than to the survival of the church.

For this to become a reality, the body of Christ must be in a right relationship with its Head. Each individual member should function as God intends and be filled with the supernatural power of the Holy Spirit. But until religion is exposed for what it is and its hold over many Christians broken, then these hopes are no more than idealistic dreams. The axe has to be laid to the roots of all religiosity (Mt 3:10).

7

Training up Leaders

Roger Ellis

Roger Ellis leads Pioneer South, a network of churches in one of the regions with which Pioneer is involved. Working with an emerging team he is involved in church planting, leadership training and teaching. He also leads the Revelation Church based in Chichester, numbering 550. Roger is married to Margaret and they have a young daughter.

The church's profile in Britain has changed considerably in recent years. Despite an overall decline, the Holy Spirit has given fresh impetus, energy and life which means that the church is more streamlined, better equipped and poised to take its place as an agent for change in society at large.

Renewal and restoration have, in many places, created a hunger after God and a desire to be active and significant in his service. However, I have to say that activism without training equals embarrassment! If the enthusiasm generated within our churches is not carefully channelled into a positive experience of serving the Lord, disappointment, disillusionment and super-spirituality will result. As churches we have two options. Either we turn to older denominational systems of training, or we move to pioneer bold new initiatives in training and equipping people for God's service. These initiatives may well on occasions bring Bible college into the mix, but this need not necessarily be the only or even the major way that effective training can be given.

A missing factor

Despite several notable exceptions, effective training seems to be a missing ingredient within even the most successful of churches. The oft-repeated, classic scenario is the well-known, successful evangelical/charismatic church which has a large attendance every Sunday. Despite this vast people resource all its full-time staff, right from the minister through to the youth pastor, have been imported from outside. Not one of them was homegrown. On the credit side they have been able to release people to Bible college and even overseas, but in debit body ministry has been relegated to the sharing of spiritual 'bits' in meetings. The ministry of the church is not truly team based because a professional and élitest approach to ministry prevails.

The vast army of church attenders have become little more than renewed pew fodder. They are likely to remain in this unhealthy, inactive state until the leaders wake up and invest strategically in motivating, training and equipping people locally to be involved in the work of God.

Surely this is possible? Is it not true that *all* ministry whether evangelistic, pastoral or teaching should, at even the basic level, be able to reproduce after its own? This, I believe, should be our aim and goal. The rest of this chapter will contain some brief ideas as to how this may be worked out in the local situation.

The nature of discipleship

Too many of our discipling efforts seem to be geared to making good little church members rather than releasing folk into a life of usefulness in God—serving him and seeking first the kingdom. A disciple is a learner, being transformed, sanctified, empowered and equipped. No matter how long we have been Christians we will always be disciples (learners) and so will always be learning and changing. One of the characteristics of Christian maturity is therefore constant change. The fact is that God wants putty, not well-taught, spiritually-gifted rocks!

Jesus' disciples followed him (Mt 4:18–20) and travelled with him, learning (being taught) in both public and private forums (Mt 13:1–23). He gave them opportunity (Lk 10:1–16), and taught them how to cope with success and how to learn amid failure (Mk 9:14–29). He dealt with their attitudes and character (Mt 20:20–28), their basic motivation and allowed them to experience truth first hand for themselves (Mt 16:16–17). He dealt with them firmly when they needed it (Mt 16:22–23). He nurtured them, cared for them, prayed for them (Lk 22:31–32) and his investment saw them through the traumas of his death into the joy of his resurrection and their empowering at Pentecost.

The Apostle Paul seemed to follow a similar model with his trainees. He cared for them in a fatherly manner (2 Tim 1:2), and they travelled with him experiencing on-the-job training. Alongside this, it is clear that he imparted gifting and ministry to them through training and the laying on of hands (Tit 1:5; 2 Tim 1:6–7). This is the kind of discipling that equips people for service, leadership and usefulness rather than for inactivity and a self-indulgent faith. People's gifts and talents are harnessed for God's kingdom and not just left to be squandered in ways that do not advance the broad purposes of God. Surely this discipleship is for all Christians and not just a chosen minority of activists?

Of course, these New Testament models of discipleship have historical roots in both Judaism and the Old Testament which we have no space to explore here. However, it should be noted that these models differ considerably to much of the Greek-style, knowledge based system that prevails in Christian teaching today. I believe that if we could only learn some basic lessons from this on-the-job, lifestyle training then our church life could be considerably enhanced.

The best place for it!

Of course it is easy to look at what the church isn't doing without offering any remedy for the situation. However, looking on the bright side I feel we need to appreciate that the church can be the ideal community within which training can occur. Let us briefly explore just some of the reasons why this is so.

Motivation

As Christians we have been *individually called* (Rom 1:7) and God has prepared good works for us to do in advance of our rising to the challenge of this calling (Eph 2:10). Every believer is gifted, has the gift of the Holy Spirit and can be used both supernaturally and otherwise in God's service. It is what we are here for!

However, the church is also *corporately called*. Individually we are but disembodied limbs, but together we are the body of Christ (1 Cor 12:12–31). Individually we are temples of the Holy Spirit (1 Cor 6:19), but corporately we are a more powerful and glorious temple which has a greater destiny (Eph 2:11–22).

The church can be a body within which people are educated and motivated both for and by God's purposes. Our corporate power and impact are greater than the sum total of the individual parts if we were left to our own devices. We need to become communities that are dynamic, motivating, redeeming, commissioning and sending—in line with those who took the gospel to the ends of civilisation during New Testament times.

Obviously training without motivation is impossible. People will neither learn nor grow in God if they haven't been enthused by the Holy Spirit. It is therefore extremely important to let loose ministries that are exhortative, dynamic and motivational in the church. Nice, polite, maintenance-style ministry will not do the job but will need to be on hand afterwards to provide a context for development and channel the enthusiasm when half the congregation want to leave their jobs *now* and move to Africa!

Environment

Alongside motivation the church is the ideal environment for growth and training. So much of the training Jesus gave his disciples was earthed in relationship, friendship and sharing as they ate, drank and lived together. The church ideally should be relationships, friendship and community—the perfect environment for Jesus-style leadership training.

Friendship is never meant to be self-indulgent, but is supposed to be inclusive of others, promoting growth, maturity, training and development in the church (Eph 4:15–16). Exhortation, rebuke, encouragement and comfort are the 'stuff' of church life and the means by which growth is secured, and real, honest relationships are established.

Fellowship that is actually going somewhere is friendship that is mutually resourcing, shaping one another for service and provoking one another to good works that advance God's kingdom.

Resources (potentially!)

Friendship, relationship and community are vital, but the church is shaped by and founded around God-given ministries (Eph 2:19–22; 4:11–16). No local church is an island and complete in and of itself. We all need the influence and resources of the wider body and I'll explore ways in which we've worked this out practically later.

However, most churches have some, or, more rarely, all of the ministries in either mature, developing or embryonic form. We can't work with what we haven't got, only with what we have. So let us stop bemoaning the lack of resources and get on with it!

Development costs

If we are to be transformed into training, equipping and releasing communities, a price will have to be paid. When a factory prepares for the production of a new innovation it must first invest much expense and time in 'tooling up'. That is reorganising the production line and installing the new machinery for the job. So it is in the church context. Our priorities and finances will need adjusting and structures will need to be trimmed. Old machinery that has served us well in the past will have to be scrapped to make room for the new.

One fellowship I know of had been in existence for over ten years and had many people who had been trained, nurtured and pastored for that whole period of time. Yet the church was low on people who could take key positions of leadership and function; a situation which required a radical response. Their solution was to scrap house groups completely, keeping people in nurture/pastoral groups for the first eighteen months after conversion, or if they needed specific care. The rest of the church was divided into training and action groups, each with a specific brief and responsibility. This was a clear break from the conventional house-group system, which has produced much fruit in this particular context.

Alongside structural inconvenience the current leaders will need to submit themselves to the pains of delegation. This initially involves more work than if you did the job yourself and will consist of letting people make mistakes, watching them do a worse job than you would and resisting the temptation to take responsibility back when it suits you. This aspect of leadership training has driven me up the wall on many occasions!

Sadly, there are few leaders around who are prepared to endure this and many are content to play safe, opting for a system of 'one-man ministry with a few helping out'. This is hardly going to produce the kind of leadership that is needed to take the church to the year 2000 and beyond.

Practical modules

The setting up of training courses can be a time-consuming and expensive task. There is a need, therefore, to maximise all available resources. Within our church we have six congregations which still retain the 'one church' identity. While the pastoral issues are resolved locally within congregations, we maximise our resources by doing all our training and operating our Evangelism, Social Action, Media, Worship (etc) teams on an overall basis. This is more cost effective and also makes it a more worthwhile proposition to draw in quality ministry from outside.

At a much wider level, within Pioneer, we have drawn together our varying resources for a number of training projects. One of these is TIE (Training In Evangelism) Teams which has sought to merge the benefits of intensive, centralised Evangelism Training modules with on-the-ground experience and practice in a local situation. So far it has proved very effective.

I will now outline below some of the various training modules we've used in our local situation, hoping they will be useful to you as you formulate your own.

Leadership training programme

We would put all our potential leaders, house-group leaders and those who are moving towards some form of responsibility through this course. It has also been a resource to a number of other churches in our area who are regularly channelling people into it. The course covers a period of six to eight months, giving time for the material to be 'earthed' on the ground. A tutorial system is set up in order that each participant can work through the issues raised, have particular projects set and in some cases do appropriate written work.

Sessions we have used include:

PART 1—WHAT IS LEADERSHIP?
 (1) Introduction to biblical leadership
 (2) Authority and accountability
 (3) Dealing with leadership pressure and handling your personal life
 (4) The leader as shepherd
 (5) Delegation, representation and teamwork
 (6) Counselling and confrontation
 (7) Servanthood and responsibility
 (8) Embodying and imparting the vision and ethos of the church

(9) Healing and deliverance

PART 2—LEADING A SMALL GROUP

(10) Leading your house group into evangelism
(11) Creativity and spiritual gifts
(12) Teaching and discussions
(13) Caring for new Christians
(14) Faith-filled planning and preparation
(15) Conclusions and assessments (including feedback on the course)

Preachers'/public speakers' training

There are two courses we have run either alternatively or alongside one another. One is for those who show signs of a definite preaching/teaching gift and the other for those who are not called to give talks, but nevertheless are used publicly in meetings, be it prophetically or otherwise.

Sessions include:

What is communication?
Cross-cultural communication
A written project
Preaching from content
Styles of teaching (prophetic, exhortative, exegetical)

We also do two practical sessions. One where members of the group are individually given fifteen minutes to prepare a five-minute talk on, say, 'Dealing with terrorism' and they then give their talk to the group and share feedback. Alongside this we have a video evening when each person gives a short talk and then has the joy of observing themselves and learning from it. Prayer for insecurity is offered at the end of each meeting!

Also, certain trainees are given the opportunity to preach in one of our congregations. A biblical subject will be debated in the group and the talk structure developed together. One trainee will go away, prepare the talk and bring it back to the leader for shaping up, adding illustrations and helping with humour, etc. It is then preached on the Sunday and feedback with encouragement is given by the group at the next meeting.

Theology action group

This is designed to get people thinking basically about the theological issues that face the church and society. Sessions have included:

Biblical authority and inspiration
Biblical interpretation
The cults and their Scripture-twisting
Biblical overview
Enlarging your vocabulary (biblical word study)
Church history
Doctrinal hotcakes of the past and present

We try to use as much interaction and workshop material as possible to make it more accessible to the less intellectually minded. In future those who are interested will be encouraged to produce short papers on specific issues.

Management and resource team

This is a course designed to form a team to deal with managing events, projects, administration, tape ministry, etc. Sessions have included:

The heart and cost of servanthood
Keeping good lines of communication
Accountability
Representing one another
Organising an event
Working as a team (including delegation skills)
Diary and time management
Handling pressure situations

Social action

This has been, as it suggests, more action than theory. As people get involved it enlarges their heart for God's kingdom and stretches their caring and people skills. Initially we appointed different people in the group to investigate the needs present in our area. We contacted voluntary bodies like Mencap, Citizens' Advice Bureau, Help the Aged, local hospitals, local hospices, WRVS and the Social Services.

We then had to ask what our available resources were. Their limited nature meant we could only at present achieve short, one-off projects. These have included:

(1) Specific tasks given by the Social Services. For instance, we have cleared gardens, decorated rooms and helped with cooking and shopping.

(2) We have raised money for the local hospice.

(3) We have taken old people from a home on a minibus journey and to the pub!

(4) We have helped a children's home with setting up a chicken run and with their crop rotation, working for semi-self-sufficiency and the setting up of a profitable village shop.

(5) The group is also investigating the issue of Christian Citizenship and producing a paper on it for the church.

(6) We have launched a local 'Care For Romania' which has sent three trips to Romania, refurbished orphanages, provided medical equipment and raised finance through persuading local businesses to sponsor these initiatives. The combined value of the finance and equipment provided is over £30,000.

In the future we hope this group will lead the whole church into community involvement.

Foundation Course: training pastors

Within the context of our Foundation Course for new believers, we try to impart pastoral skills to some of our members who are keen to be used. They attend the group alongside its leaders and are given two or three of the group to see regularly, to befriend them and to care for them. Under supervision, they lead parts of the meeting and the leader sets them tasks in prayer and advises on issues to talk and pray through with the new Christians. They see at least one person weekly for a meal and report back weekly on progress made.

This has proved a great opportunity for folk to get involved either prior to or after our leadership training course. It is also good experience for our trainee evangelists to see what happens after a person comes to Christ and how to help lead them forward. Because of the ongoing and progressive nature of this course it is also a good opportunity for trainees to work alongside a skilled pastor, who will be clearly shaping them and helping them to develop.

Media training and action group

This is something that we have now let drop in the context of the church. However, in the past we have trained people in:

Writing letters to local media on specific issues
How to produce press releases
Publicity for events and publicity photographs

They were also involved with building relationships with the local media, running hospital radio and investigating community radio and local radio. People from this group were also involved in launching the Chichester Care For Romania project and are also looking into the whole area of a high-profile, fund-raising event for the Mayor's charity, which could raise funding and also the profile of the church in the community.

Evangelism team

Here we have trained and produced an ongoing evangelism team which works in all our congregations. Their responsibility is to lead the whole church in evangelism and to be a resource for our evangelistic events. They engage in regular streetwork, have experienced youth work, door-to-door work and some of them are taken into both schools and local prisons on a regular basis.

Their training has included:

Street Drama
Street Preaching

Telling Your Story (testimony)
Spiritual Warfare in Evangelism
Praise and Worship in Evangelism
Power Evangelism
Engaging Conversation
Leading Someone to Christ
Dealing with the Difficult Questions

They have produced evangelistic material as well as a video-based Just Looking Group. Also, members have produced an evangelism training pack which they have presented around all the church house groups to stimulate evangelism.

Counselling course

This has been arranged alongside three other churches in our area and is designed to equip our pastors and house-group leaders to move up a level in their ability to cope with the more difficult pastoral cases. Subjects covered include:

Deliverance
Caring for the Whole Person
Ministering in the Power of the Holy Spirit
Being Clothed in Your Right Mind
Sexual Problems
Natural and Social Problems
Marriage Growth and Development
Dealing with Self-Image Problems
Caring in the Crisis Situation
Caring Beyond the Crisis

These sessions will include a balance of Bible teaching, practical advice, workshop material and also question times.

Equipped to lead

This is an in-depth training course we have run in Pioneer designed to provide theological training for those in local church eldership or in key areas of ministry. The course operates over a year, being one day a month with one whole weekend away during the year. This course seeks to look at issues in depth and to provide Bible-college-style training in the local church context.

Issues covered include:

The Doctrines of God, Man and Salvation
Eschatology
Exegesis and Hermeneutics
Sexuality
The Church and Family
Divorce and Remarriage

We are also launching 'Equipped to Lead 2' which will be one-off day seminars for those who have been through the 'Equipped to Lead 1' course. These seminars will take some of the issues we have already covered, but go into greater depth as well as covering some new and relevant issues.

Emerging leaders' forum

This is a day every eight to twelve weeks for all the emerging young full-time leaders in the Pioneer network. It is a time for teaching, discussion and shaping people up in their conceptual understanding of church life and ministry. Alongside this we seek to give them quality time with key older leaders during which there can be ministry, sharing and general personal help for them. There is also a good length of time for friendship as well as questions and discussion on issues that affect those who are full time. The main aim of this time is that through prayer, sharing, teaching and interaction new key ministries can be developed in their character and quality.

School of prophecy

This is an ongoing school running a course that is open-ended in its length. Meeting once a month, some of the courses have still being going on after a couple of years. It is designed to teach about the whole area of prophetic ministry as well as developing people's character and gradually to see a mature understanding and practice of the prophetic gift developed in our churches.

These are just some of the ideas we have pursued. The local, area and national church has vast potential. Our available resources at grass-roots level are vast and largely untapped. However, if we want visibility in our nation we must first gain credibility. This credibility will be built as we allow our churches to become vibrant, training, discipling and equipping communities. My motto is therefore: 'If it moves, train it!'

8

Women—Frozen Assets

Christine Noble

Christine Noble has been a pioneer for women in leadership and ministry. She has spoken at a wide range of women's meetings, leadership events and conferences. She has contributed to several articles on women in leadership and ministry for national magazines and has written a book on women in the church. She has a longing for the arts to be restored to the church.

Almost a decade ago now, as I was preparing for a weekend away with the women from my own church, my husband John had a vision for us. It was a very simple vision, but extremely telling. He saw the assets of the church, as represented by the men, lying about in the sun, slowly rotting. Those of the women, however, were in a deep freeze, solid ice, unusable unless thawed out.

This almost needs no interpretation, but for the sake of clarity I will explain it to you. The assets rotting in the sun sums up the male attitude often found, not only in church, but at home, work and play. Men feel they can do anything they like to set their minds to, once they actually get up and get going. The unfortunate truth is, however, only small numbers do 'get up and get going', hence the 'rotting'. The frozen assets represent all the gifts, abilities, drive and radical thoughts to be found in women. They are all there, but unavailable unless the climate completely changes.

Although few would deny that we are experiencing a leadership crisis, and have been for some time, there still seems to be an expectation on a wide scale that male seniority and leadership are synonymous. This totally ignores the obvious abilities in young people and women.

That vision came at least ten years ago. At about the same time, I remember having a conversation with one of my friends about women in leadership. The gist of the conversation was that basically he accepted me as the 'exception which proves the rule'. My reply, coming from conviction and faith, was, 'Watch yourself being buried under exceptions over the next decade!' Sadly, I have to confess that my words, as yet, have not come true. Yes, there are a few balmy and sunny areas, but much is still arctic, wintry and frozen.

1990 saw the publication of my book *What in the World Is God Saying about Women?* My hope was that people would begin to wake up to the fact that, even where there is correct theology, few women are employed in ministry and leadership. Theology is not enough to liberate people, there also has to be much work done in the hurting areas in our lives. In the book (pages 36–37) I wrote:

> In the church we have been taught that it was the woman who was deceived and is therefore more gullible and in danger of being misled. This sin disqualifies her from certain areas of activity in the life and work of the church. Even supposing this idea were completely true, where do forgiveness and redemption come in? My Bible teaches me that my sins, although blood red, shall be as white as snow. Restoration accompanies forgiveness so that I can function fully as my Father intended. Anyway, man also sinned. In fact, in Romans 5:12–21, Paul puts the responsibility for sin squarely on Adam's shoulders. It could be argued that his sin was the greater, for he was not deceived but acted in the full knowledge of what he was doing. God spoke to him and instructed him personally in the Garden before the woman was formed.

> With this seeming bias against women in the church, does this mean that disparity begins here at the cross? Are we saying that God's judgements are purely on the basis of sex and have nothing to do with the severity of the sin? On the contrary, the Bible does not give us this understanding. God is consistently righteous and true in all his ways. I

know that we humans find it almost impossible not to grade sin. We even find comfort in the fact that the crimes of others seem worse than ours, but God sees sin for what it is. His punishments are just and he is equally forgiving when faced with a repentant heart. So where does the concept of a disqualification in the case of women come from? Has the Lord made an exception as far as deception is concerned? Is deception the one sin for which restoration can never be complete? And what of men who are deceived?

As a result of this attitude, women tend to spend too much time examining every contribution they might want to make. This often results in the moment passing, which only reinforces for them the inevitability of them having got it wrong anyway. With all this going on inside them, it is easy to understand why so often they are unable to cope with even the slightest criticism.

I come from the stream now known as the 'New Churches'. Here the 'thaw' has been going on for some time. In fact among the women in this stream there seems to be, at times, a naïveté of attitude about what is going on outside of their protected environment. Let me cite you an up-to-date, personal experience. For some years now, certain team leaders have been meeting together for fellowship, friendship and discussion. It was decided, because this had been so good, to open up this time to senior ministries on those teams. A date was set, a venue arranged and, as a senior ministry on two of these teams, I was invited. Now I'm not daft, or blind to the many and varied attitudes towards women in my situation, so I went, like a returning spacecraft, with my heat shield in place in order to prevent burn up. It was just as well I did.

We travelled in my car, so as we were finding it difficult to park, I dropped the men off and went further afield to find a parking spot. When I eventually entered the building on my own, one of the first questions I was asked was, 'Whose secretary are you?' Quite a gross assumption as I can neither spell nor type, and couldn't administrate my way out of a paper bag. I successfully fielded that one and went on in. The proceedings hadn't as yet got underway, so I collected a cup of coffee and introduced myself to people I hadn't met before and chatted and exchanged news with those I did know. When we were called to order, I sat with the people I was talking to and the session began. Later I had to move the car and on returning everyone had been broken down into groups for discussion, so I joined myself to a group. At lunchtime, we were asked to stagger our departure for the dining room, to prevent a clog-up at the self-service tables. When my group's turn came, I obediently went with them to get my food. Part way through lunch the fellow sitting opposite me asked if he might ask me a question. Checking my heat shield was in place, just in case my tongue got the better of me if I didn't like the question, I answered, 'Of course.'

'Why didn't you sit with your husband during the morning session?' he asked.

My inclination was to say, 'Why should I? We're not Siamese twins.' I didn't weaken however, but I asked him a question in response. 'Did you sit with the people you were talking to at the time the meeting was called to order?'

'Yes,' was his answer.

'Well, so did I,' was my response. I didn't say anything more, so there was a silence, then simply the word 'Oh!' and the subject was changed.

That was not an end to it, however. I went to the food table for some reason—more coffee I think. There was a restraining hand on my arm and, 'Do you mind if I ask you a question?'

Heat shield in place? Yes. 'Not at all.'

'Why didn't you sit with your husband for lunch?'

I did think this was a bit thick and I think my answer came out a little sharply. 'We weren't in the same group, so either he would have to leave his, as mine went in first, or I would have had to hang around for his to be dismissed. It seemed only logical to go with my group to the dining room and eat my meal as we had all been asked to do.'

Three questions in one day from those who are meant to be among the more avant-garde of the church. Just as a footnote to this occurrence, when John and I compared notes, no one had said anything to him, not even the concerned gentleman in question. I wonder why? The thaw is extremely patchy.

What then do women have to offer which is different from what men have to offer? In order to answer my own question, I shall need to generalise. Men in the main tend to be logical, outward-looking, reasoning and scientific. Women, however, tend to be creative, protective, intuitive and artistic. Men will weigh up all the pros and cons in a situation, gather all the relevant information, and on the basis of all the facts decide what action to take in the near future. Women will look at all the data, understand the reasoning (sometimes), but feel action needs to be taken now, if not yesterday. Both, when moving in the sphere of their gifting in God, can be wonderfully, earth-changingly right! Both, when missing the Holy Spirit's touch, can be devastatingly wrong.

All of these attributes are to be found in God, and the Bible teaches us that we are 'fearfully and wonderfully made' (Ps 139) because we are made in his image. Without all of our gifts firing on all cylinders, we are deficient and not yet totally a reflection of our Creator. We need one another. You do obviously have men and women who belong in the opposite category. This doesn't make them strange and ill-gotten, just different from the majority. If however you do have a problem with the more 'feminine' side of creation, it could cause you some difficulties. I quote again from my book.

If we continue to misunderstand God's intention with gender; should a man hold to male authority or even superiority, with leadership in the church being exclusively male, this very attitude itself will foster within him feelings of thankfulness for his manliness in a rather specific way. Even though this is unconscious it will almost certainly be there. Like the Jews I mentioned earlier, our Christian men will end up thanking God for making them male, and believing, even if it is unspoken, that to be female is undesirable. Under these circumstances, for a man to discover even a trace of femininity in himself would be completely unacceptable. However, no one living is either totally masculine or totally feminine; each has an element of the other in a variety of strengths of expressions. Pride and fear will be the outcome of such views, and these will be more than enough to maintain the barriers between the sexes. God did not build a clear wall of partition.

We can see this in the way the church is described in Scripture. The role of the church in the world is to be the body of Christ. We are his body, so in that sense we are clearly masculine. The role of the church to Christ himself is that of a bride. Here we become totally feminine. The virgin bride coming to maturity and readiness is waiting for Christ, the Bridegroom, to return so that together they can enjoy the greatest wedding feast of all time. In relation to the enemy, the church becomes an army. Armies historically are heavily weighted on the masculine side, but not exclusively so. We have seen with Deborah and Jael that there is a place for women in warfare. The army then contains both elements. Finally, we see the church's role to the Father and to the Holy Spirit as that of a temple, a dwelling place for God which is neutral.

Christ is not returning for a male-dominated and orientated church, but for an integrated body, where he will see his own reflection, with all its apparent opposites, supernaturally blended into the rainbow-coloured wisdom of God spoken of in Ephesians 3.

Having now been part of Gerald Coates' Pioneer Team for some months, it has been good to feel not only accepted but also affirmed by the men on that team. When I told them what happened to me at the teams' day, which I wrote about earlier, there was everything from shocked unbelief to conviction that I was pulling their legs. I'm very happy to say there was absolutely no laughter. They didn't find it funny, just unbelievable. Martin Scott has in fact taken time to do a theological study on Pioneer's perspective on women in leadership and ministry for those who are interested in following this matter through. I haven't in any way attempted to do this here, but this paper is available through the Pioneer Office, PO Box 79c, Esher, Surrey KT10 9LP, England.

In Galatians 3:26–29 it says:

You are all sons of God through faith in Christ Jesus, for all of you who were baptised into Christ have been clothed with Christ. There is neither Jew nor Greek, slave nor free, male nor female, for you are all one in Christ Jesus. If you belong to Christ, then you are Abraham's seed, and heirs according to the promise.

If I were a feminist, which I'm not, I could be side-tracked into a debate over the male-orientated translation of this scripture. However, as one of the heirs, and a firstborn son at that (they get the largest share), I rejoice that in Christ there are no divisions of any sort. In the natural world I am a white, middle-class English woman, but in Jesus I am an heir. Praise God! We on the Pioneer Team are dedicated to liberating people from any restriction brought about by their race, class or gender. The way forward in the 1990s is to be part of a team, running the race where the first prize is men, women and children for God.

Let's go for gold.

9
The Need for Team

Kevin Allan

Kevin Allan leads the City Gate Church in Southampton and oversees several other churches in the Solent area on behalf of the Pioneer Team. He is on the editorial team for Pioneer magazine and was instrumental in overseeing the first national conference of Pioneer Churches, 'Breaking the Mould'. Kevin is married to Sue and they have two children, Matthew and Jessica.

The preacher continued boldly, 'And now I am a Christian, my life has purpose.' He paused for effect, but unfortunately the brief silence was broken by a voice from the rear of the auditorium.

'What is it then?'

'What is it then,' returned the startled preacher. 'What is it then,' he repeated, but in a higher pitch. There was a further pause before he garbled his reply, trotting out a whole list of religious-sounding phrases and clichés, but for me the point had already been beautifully made.

I may be a Christian and so have an eternal destiny, freedom from sin and guilt, and a wonderful relationship with my Father in heaven. Indeed, I have infinitely more going for me than the average man in the street, aimlessly pursuing as much satisfaction and pleasure as he can until he draws his last breath. Yet to say I have purpose, without ever taking the time to assess what exactly that purpose may be, is perhaps a trifle vague or even smug.

The words of the Apostle Paul came flooding back to me. 'Therefore I do not run like a man running aimlessly; I do not fight like a man beating the air' (1 Cor 9:26). It was obvious that Paul, for one, was a man of purpose with clearly-defined goals and objectives, so I determined to be like him, not only having specific aims, but devising a strategy to achieve those aims.

The emergence of team ministry today

I happen to be one of the new breed of Christians who have been saved and grown up in what many now refer to as 'New Church'. As such, I have tasted very little of traditional churches and their structures, many of which would, in my opinion, appear to belong to the age of the dinosaur. Yet how quickly the new, supposedly radical, churches can fall foul of the same kind of inflexibility.

For all my Christian life, house groups have been the main framework of church. Somehow these smaller groups meeting in homes were able to translate my faith into an everyday language, afford a certain amount of real pastoral care and accountability, and create a forum to develop friendship and relationships within the body of Christ. This is, of course, stating the obvious to many, especially to those who have been part of such a group for a considerable time. But the question has to be asked, 'Surely there is more to church than house-group meetings?'

This issue first came to my notice a few years back, when somebody had the audacity to say to me that they were bored with my house-group meetings. When they then went on to say that they would rather watch *EastEnders*, I knew a rigorous appraisal was in order!

The truth of the matter was, of course, that some of the people in the fellowship had been in house groups for the best part of ten years and had subsequently attained a certain measure of maturity in their faith. They had now reached the stage where the prospect of another house-group meeting had become so dull that they were maliciously racking their brains prior to the meeting to construct some kind of problem, simply to liven up the evening's proceedings.

What was the point of maintaining meetings of this format for such people? Clearly none at all. Their predicament could be likened to that of a student of one of those rather more obscure subjects taught at our universities or higher education institutions. The only possible outlet for their newly-acquired knowledge would be if, in the fullness of time, they in turn could teach it, so perpetuating a rather ridiculous circle. For many of those in house groups, the only possible release for their ministry and usefulness would be if, at some future date, they would be considered able enough to lead their own group.

Now do not get me wrong. It is not my intention to malign such a responsibility. Indeed, if a house group or similar structure is able to give a foundation, particularly to new converts, and provide a setting for care, prayer and friendship among God's people, then it serves a very useful purpose. My point is this: new structures are continually necessary if the church is to move forward.

Today there is a fresh emphasis running through the Christian community of this land. It is about turning outward the blessings we have received from God; it is about boldness and pushing back the tide of secular humanism; it is about being a voice in an age of great need. Much of this emphasis can be gleaned from the pages of this book. To meet this challenge, new structures and administration are necessary.

The role of house groups has been primarily to care and maintain, and so is essentially passive. What is needed are structures that are designed for a specific purpose, to do a job of work. It is against this background that the concept of team ministry has emerged. All across the country, teams of people have been coming together to work towards defined ends and specific goals. Teams with specified lifespans to achieve specific tasks. Teams to pursue certain areas of ministry and burden. Above all, teams created for a purpose and not for passivity.

Team—a biblical perspective

It was at a Christian Bible week that I noted the conversation of a rather irate young man. 'Friendship!' he ranted angrily. 'Friendship! All you charismatics seem to talk about is friendship. Show me where it talks about friendship in the Bible!'

Well of course to the simple-minded, if you look the word up in a fat concordance, you would have a thin result. The fact that the spirit and dynamic of friendship screams at you from nearly every page of the New Testament is completely irrelevant if you are bogged down in a simplistic approach.

Similarly, the word 'team' is not falling off every page of Scripture. In fact my *Cruden's Concordance* draws a complete blank. Yet very clearly the dynamic of team was an ever-present phenomenon in the ministry of Jesus and the formation of the early church. The best model of all is when Jesus himself called the twelve to be his team. So crucial is this event in our understanding of team, that it merits some further attention.

When Jesus called his disciples, they were anything but useful team members. Mark's Gospel tells us that Jesus was walking beside the Sea of Galilee and he saw Simon Peter and his brother Andrew casting a net into the lake. Then Jesus said to them, 'Come, follow me . . . and I will make you fishers of men' (Mk 1:17).

The key word here is 'make'. At this point in time Simon Peter and Andrew had no grasp of the kingdom of God, signs and wonders, the teaching of Jesus, or even whether he was the Messiah. They were simply raw material with a certain amount of potential. Even at the end of the most intensive three-year training programme imaginable, Peter at the crucial moment denied any association with Jesus (Mt 26:69–75).

If this had been Peter's final examination after his three-year course, then he would have failed miserably. Yet, just a few weeks later, he had risen from those desperate depths to become the clear leader among the believers and proceeded to preach a sermon to the multitudes which resulted in some three thousand being saved and added to the church in a single day (Acts 2:14–41).

The dismal failure Peter tasted a few days previously was perhaps his greatest lesson of all, for it equipped him with a true understanding of the love and grace of God. An essential part of team ministry is not just the purpose and end it has been created to fulfil, but the formation and development of those in the team to enable them to achieve those purposes with ever-increasing effectiveness.

Training and development

If you and I are intending to be part of any team, we must be prepared to be trained and developed along the way. For Peter and the rest of the disciples, this development happened in the best school of all—the school of life. Not for them a three-year course at the Galilean School of Christian Studies. For the disciples, it was a case of listening to the teaching of Jesus as he preached to the masses; it was questions and answers as they walked and travelled together; and, most importantly, it was observing the example and ministry of Jesus at work, and then being told to go out and do likewise.

When I was involved in a college course of applied economics, somebody gave a definition of the subject matter as 'common sense made difficult'. What an apt description that would be for much of the endless circle of analysis that masquerades as Christian education and development.

Now there is, of course, no substitute for good teaching, but when Jesus taught his disciples, it was on the move, in location. That is the kind of radical schooling I enjoy, and that is why team ministry is so exciting, because it cuts both ways—outwardly in the purpose the team has been formed for, with its specific aims and objectives; inwardly in the formation and development of the personnel involved.

There is an unhelpful trait evolving within many of the newer churches in recent years which I would describe as 'perfection paranoia'. Clearly certain responsibilities demand a certain level of Christian maturity, but how one measures that necessary level of maturity and standing can sometimes prove very difficult.

However, I am convinced there are many more people who need to be released into team ministry and responsibility. If we have to wait until somebody is perfect before they are given an area of function, for fear of the consequences of such action, then we may find we have a very long wait.

Such a fear (perfection paranoia) can be a real stumbling-block to church growth. Of course wisdom needs to be employed in such decisions, but when you look in detail at the weaknesses, selfishness and flaws that were evident in Jesus' selected team, I do find a measure of reassurance and hope for us today. There will always be disappointment and failure, but Jesus did handle Judas rather well, and it did not seem to affect his mission adversely.

When I look back over my own history, I see an ill-prepared young man of twenty-three years, thrust into the forefront of a small team of leaders which had to take on the task of a fellowship of forty or so young people, most with a multitude of problems. But circumstances and events demanded that I took it on, so I did. With the gift of hindsight, I am not sure that I would choose to give such a person in similar circumstances that kind of responsibility. Yet that experience was very formative for me, and the fellowship has more than survived to tell the tale.

Therefore, for my part, I do not want to overprotect people by holding them back from responsibility and ministry, if it is that very responsibility which will be the formative factor in bringing them to maturity in Christ. Besides, a beauty of team ministry is that it minimises the risk of disaster because there are always other people available to step in and cover a person or situation should disaster strike.

Again, when I think of my own experiences as part of the Pioneer Team, it is the very nature of the responsibilities and ministry that are required to be part of that team which have brought to the surface inadequacies and insecurities in my own life. So when I wobble (as I have done on numerous occasions) others in the team have been there to cover and help me through. This has enabled me to mature and so in turn I can become a greater asset and resource to the ongoing team purposes.

Inevitably, as the responsibilities and vision of a given team develop, there will be a need to expand and subdivide to meet the challenge. Yet here again Jesus has given us an inspirational example. He realised that the kingdom would be best prospered if those in his team could go out and do the work he was performing. In Luke 9–10 we see how first with the twelve, and then with the seventy-two, Jesus broke them down into teams of two to go out and do the work of preaching the gospel and healing people everywhere.

Again the twofold effect of team ministry clearly emerges, for not only did they achieve this end, but their own lives were formed along the way. When they returned, it was with great joy that they said, 'Lord, even the demons submit to us in your name' (Lk 10:17).

In the Acts of the Apostles, we read how on one occasion Paul, Barnabas and John were sent off as a team to spread the good news about Jesus (Acts 13:5). On another occasion it was Paul, Silas and Timothy who went from town to town visiting the churches, seeing them strengthened in faith and growing daily (Acts 16:1–5). Different teams to achieve different objectives in different locations, but all serving the over-riding purpose of glorifying God.

If we need biblical precedents, there are many to be found. Team ministry was clearly a New Testament reality, and likewise it surely must be a reality in the church of today.

Being part of a team

The reason why team ministry is being emphasised in the way that it is today is that it is the most effective way of getting the job done. In the short term a team that is properly functioning can still achieve far more corporately than the sum of its members' individual efforts. In the longer term, however, that potential is dramatically increased because of the consequential interaction and development of the team members.

But team ministry does carry a price tag, for it demands a

measure of self-sacrifice and discipline, particularly in the area of personal ambition. For one of the necessary requirements is that personal goals are compatible with the team goals. If they are not compatible, some personal goals may need to be put to one side for the sake of the team. Fortunately, God's economy is of a different order to that of the world's, and he has a strange way of bringing honour and reward to those who make such a sacrifice.

For a team to be effective, everyone must own the team goals, otherwise it is a team in name only. The successful team will comprise those who are using their gifts and abilities to assist the team effort. If a member has no suitable gift, then we must question their inclusion.

My definition of team would be simply this: 'Two or more people moving on a path of interaction and relationship towards a common goal.' The disqualification for team is equally straightforward: 'Two out of three owning this common goal is not enough!' This is probably why Solomon in his wisdom wrote, 'A cord of three strands is not quickly broken' (Eccles 4:12).

To be men and women of relationship may not be an essential of successful team ministry in the eyes of the world, but in Christian circles it has to be highly desirable. I am not sure that the cabinet at 10 Downing Street is made up of men and women of relationship; of those who would gladly lay down their ministry for the sake of the team effort; those who desperately want to see others succeed even at the cost of their own ambition. But we acknowledge that it does function adequately.

There is, however, always a danger when we seek to transfer worldly models and structures into the church. Of course there will be many truths and principles of secular management and team structures that are transferable, but we must never forget that the models we are pursuing as part of God's holy order will be of an altogether different flavour.

It is inconceivable to me that I would not be in some kind of positive relationship with those I am working with in a team sense. I may not have had the time to develop a deep friendship with every team member, but in as much as we are all redeemed by the same blood, filled with the same Holy Spirit and endeavouring to live by the same moral standards, we can at least be friends.

As I have already said, a beauty of team ministry is that it minimises the risk of disaster, for if an individual should cease to function, then there is always another on hand, trained and ready to stand in the breach. This dynamic does give us the opportunity to take a few risks in team selection. Judas was a risk. I am not of the opinion that he was selected by Jesus to be the one who would betray him, even though Jesus knew it was going to happen some time before the event. My personal conviction is that Judas, the zealot, could have made the grade. Sadly we know his story. So why did Jesus take such a risk? Well, you could argue that the wisdom of his selection of Peter was similarly doubtful. This wild, ill-tempered fisherman, with a tendency to be foul-mouthed, would have undoubtedly been consumed by his own weaknesses sooner or later. Yet, by the grace of God, and in the context of team, those weaknesses were covered by those around, and the full measure of his potential and giftedness was able to be realised.

I am glad Peter made it, although somehow I find his failures more of an encouragement than his later success. If nothing else, his life demonstrates to us all our desperate need of God and that essential need of one another.

The day of the one-man ministry (if there ever was such a day) has clearly passed. We are a priesthood of all believers. None of us is perfect, and as we seek to surge forward and positively take ground and extend God's kingdom here on earth, all those imperfections will come to the surface. Warfare of any description brings out the very best and the very worst in people. Team ministry is the only way the worst is covered, so creating a platform for the very best.

10

Kingdom Evangelism

Pete Gilbert

Pete Gilbert is known nationally as an evangelist and an escapologist, combining the two to draw large crowds at open-air events. He has written several highly successful books for teenagers, and is based at the Revelation Church Bognor. He is married to Nicky.

How do you eat an elephant? A bite at a time, of course! And how can you sum up kingdom evangelism in one chapter? You can't. All I can begin to do is point out one or two ideas based on Scripture and my experience in full-time evangelism over the last thirteen or so years. Which by no means makes me an expert. So here goes: kingdom evangelism—a bite at a time!

Of course, there are many different *types* of evangelism, many different *situations* for evangelism, many different *ways* of doing it, and many different *kinds* of evangelists. Unfortunately, many Bible-believing churches have been evangelical by name, but not evangelistic by nature. A massive credibility gap has opened between belief and practice, and we have all too often ended up with faith without works (which is dead) (Jas 2:17). 'Evangelism the churches' way' has all too often not been 'evangelism God's way'.

117

An 'in' word

To use 'kingdom' as an adjective and simply tag it on to the word 'evangelism' may indicate that we have latched on to an 'in' word, but it doesn't mean that we have all the answers. Nor should this chapter be seen as a kind of Pioneer blueprint and manifesto for all kingdom evangelism. Put something into print and it can become fixed and unchanging. We can, by investing security and hope into ideas, structures, principles and ethos, actually forget that only God is holy. All else must be assessed by several simple criteria: (a) Is it truth? (b) Does it square with Scripture? (c) Does the Holy Spirit witness to it? (d) Is it accountable to the body (God's specific church)? (e) Does it work? In each of these areas kingdom evangelism has a marvellous knack of eradicating unreality.

Nevertheless, if we use the word 'kingdom' in relation to evangelism, or in relation to anything else for that matter (attitudes, relationships, church government, training, etc), it has to mean something. For me, kingdom evangelism has certain emphases. It has a wide definition, because the kingdom is much wider than church. God's kingdom is both present *and* coming. It is within us and yet it is still to come. Wherever Jesus (the King) gets his way, then that 'territory' is wrested from the enemy and becomes God's kingdom. This kind of evangelism will therefore include anything direct or indirect, proclamation or demonstration, that expands God's kingdom in the lives of individuals and in the structures of society. Ranging itself against injustice, tyranny, oppression, poverty, sickness and demonic manifestation, kingdom evangelism must therefore take into account battlefronts in the arts, in the media, in the government, in education, in finance, and so on. Kingdom evangelism will be at pains to provide a forum within which frontliners in these areas can be encouraged, trained, nurtured and equipped.

This will save kingdom evangelism from becoming restrictive in its methods (ie, 'You can't use drama, music or whatever because it is not in the Bible'); or survivalist in its motivation ('Let's leaflet the area once a year, hold a mission, sally forth, grab some converts, then retreat back within the safety of the church battlements'). Instead, it sees the church as the primary agent of the kingdom, but it also sees the kingdom as bigger than the church. It sees the building of the church as Jesus' responsibility (Mt 16:18), and the seeking of the kingdom as ours (Mt 6:33). However, the ultimate aim of kingdom evangelism, way beyond accruing lots of *individual* conversions, is to build/plant redeemed *communities* (the church), for Jesus on the cross had a people, the church, in heart and mind (Eph 5:25–27). This nation and others too will never be 'evangelised' by the addition of individual conversions to existing churches, but rather by the multiplication of radical church congregations planted across the land, one for every 1,000–1,500 people in the community.

Two kingdoms

Kingdom evangelism also keeps a keen focus on the fact that there are only ever two kingdoms—God's and Satan's. They are not equal and opposite (God being the Creator, Satan being a created being), but they are mutually exclusive. You never get your own kingdom ('look out for number one'), but you are in one or the other ('He who is not with me is against me'—Mt 12:30). They are also both expansionist kingdoms, constantly vying for territory in people's lives, over institutions (including churches) and over geographical regions. Kingdom evangelism is about warfare—Satan's kingdom meets God's at the point of interface, of conflict. There should be a keen awareness of spiritual warfare and of the valuable place of prayer, of praise and worship and of deliverance.

Both 'kingdom' and 'evangelism'

It is *kingdom* in that the church serves by looking and moving outward into national and international society—this is salt and light—concentrating on the kingdom values of reality, of renewal and on the radical and benevolent reign of the King through aggressive faith, active involvement and through appropriate after-care. The kingdom has no parochial eye for maintaining a certain structure or denomination, but insists that structures serve people and not vice versa, and that all structures, as all ministries (Eph 4:11–13), are growth orientated, both qualitatively and quantitatively. Kingdom also indicates that the messiahship/rulership/reign of King Jesus will be in demonstration as well as proclamation. In the kingdom of God there is no suffering, no sickness and there are certainly no demons! Jesus' mandate was always to proclaim the gospel of the kingdom and he was clear about what that involved (Mt 10) and who it involved (Mt 28:16–20). So, kingdom evangelism will involve words, works warnings and wonders!

And because it is *evangelism* it will necessarily be good news not bad. Yes, 'without the shedding of blood there is no forgiveness' (Heb 9:22). Of course, without acknowledgement of sin, there is no salvation and that is bad news. But it didn't end there, for after death comes resurrection. After Calvary, Pentecost. After confession, repentance. After guilt, cleansing. Evangelism is telling the good news. It is the gospel (*Godspell* is Old English for good news) of the kingdom. It is not just about sin; it is about salvation. It is not just about sacrifice; it is about obedience. It is not about rules; it is about relationships. It is certainly not religion, but life!

Working out the practicalities

From the beginning of creation God has been revealing himself to mankind. He can be observed and deduced from nature (Rom 1:20). He can be heard in the conscience of man. He can be read of in his library, the Bible. His people Israel were a chosen nation in that they were called for a special purpose—to embody the desires of a holy God for a holy people. When Israel failed, God narrowed the focus, and his word was lived out by his prophets in extraordinary ways (including marrying a prostitute, streaking in their Y-fronts, gazing laterally at piles of dung!). When the prophets were silenced and sometimes stoned; when they themselves sold out and prophesied 'peace, peace . . . when there is no peace' (Jer 6:14); then God finally incarnated himself in the person of Jesus Christ—the Word made flesh (Jn 1:14). 'In the past God spoke to our forefathers through the prophets at many times and in various ways, but in these last days he has spoken to us by his Son, whom he appointed heir of all things, and through whom he made the universe' (Heb 1:1–3).

And so, as you would expect, we cannot separate the good news from its carrier. Jesus only ever equated himself with two things— with God (Jn 10:30) and with the gospel (Mk 8:35). Jesus is the Good News, not only in word, but also in person (Acts 1:1). As Christians we are called to do no less than live out the good news. Practically, kingdom evangelism isn't something you *do*, it is something you *are*. It is not doing but being! That is why Jesus, in promising the Holy Spirit, said, '*Be* my witnesses,' not '*Do* my witnessing' (cf Acts 1:8). Kingdom evangelism means that we *are* good news, not that we merely *have* good news. This means, in the context of committed open relationships between you, God and others, closing the credibility gap between belief and lifestyle. As someone once said, 'I hear, I forget. I see, I remember. I do, I understand.' If your neighbour only *hears* good news then within three hours he will have forgotten 30% of it, and in three days he will have forgotten 90%. However, let him *see* good news and in three days he will have only forgotten 28%, and three days later he will have retained as much as 20%. Let him both *hear and see* good news and then after three hours he will remember 85%, and three days later 65% will still be with him.

The best definition of kingdom evangelism is also the best-known verse in the Bible—John 3:16.

For God

Kingdom evangelism starts with God; with a God-awareness from the perspective that 'the earth is the Lord's, and everything in it' (Ps 24:1). It takes the biblical view that Christians are theists and not deists. That God took the initiative in creation and that he hasn't stopped taking the initiative! He is still totally and intimately involved in his creation and hasn't just left it, clock-like, to wind down into chaos. This has practical implications for kingdom evangelism's answer to hoary old chestnuts like, 'What about suffering?' We have a God actively involved in (though not the perpetrator of) suffering, to the extent of it costing him the life of his Son Jesus. There are also implications for God's sovereignty, yet without denying individual freewill and moral choice. 'While we were still sinners' (Rom 5:8), a million miles from God, at that time 'Christ died for us' and God took the initiative. Salvation is a process (I have been saved, I am being saved, I will be saved), and it began when man fell in Eden. God hinted at his future redemptive plan with the resulting first sacrifice recorded in Scripture (Gen 3:21). God's redemptive plan began even at that stage, again through his initiative! Kingdom evangelism starts with good news that there is a God who cares and is involved.

So loved

Kingdom evangelism reflects God's heart invested in his chosen people—the church. The gospel never changes, as Jesus never changes his character (Heb 13:8). But the emphases of the gospel do. It's like British Youth For Christ's old motto 'Anchored to the Rock, Geared to the Times'. Kingdom evangelism applies aspects of good news to people and situations with a moral demand on the hearer, while making sure that we scratch where people itch. We need to ask what in the 1990s will be good news to the people of the UK? I suggest the following emphases are rooted in a biblical understanding of God's kingdom.

1. That God is a faithful Father in an age which knows little of fatherhood; where one in three marriages break down.

2. That the kingdom reconciles polarities (black and white, left and right, male and female, north and south, Protestant and Roman Catholic, etc) in an age of extremes.

3. That in an era of guilt (which populates 50% plus of our psychiatric units) the gospel of the kingdom brings forgiveness, wholeness and physical healing.

4. It releases self-control and deliverance from evil in an age of selfish hedonism.

5. It restores a vision of peace and a carefully stewarded earth to this time of international unease, nuclear stand-off and 'Green' awareness.

6. Kingdom evangelism offers to a fragmented society the model of a caring family community made possible through God's adoption.

The world

Kingdom evangelism works to understand God's desire to see the whole world saved, while realising that not everyone will be. It takes seriously 2 Peter 3:9. That is why, by the end of this millennium, we in Pioneer long to see every person in the country reached with the gospel over and over again. Kingdom evangelism looks to infiltrate at every level of society. Jesus' command in Matthew 28:19 to 'go and make disciples of all nations' (not wait for them to come to us) means *all* people groups. So, kingdom evangelism will always have a local outworking, a national servant heart and an international perspective. It will look to give people away, not to keep and maintain them. It will be inclusive and not exclusive.

Practically, it will identify the people groups we all have contact with:

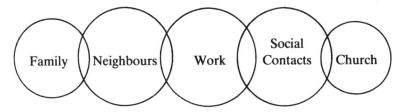

It will target them first. For while God wants the whole world saved, we can't change everyone's life everywhere, but we can change someone's life somewhere! It's like a hot plate dispenser in a self-service canteen: take off the top plate and the next one pops up; take off one friend into the kingdom of God and the next one pops up to be witnessed to!

That he gave his only Son Jesus Christ

The centre of the verse John 3:16 and the centre of the gospel, and of kingdom evangelism, is Jesus. But the real Jesus—the man not the stereotype. The man of his time—friend of sinners, frequenter of parties, provider of wine at weddings, most invited at suppers and meals, breaker of religious traditions, restorer of the role of women, worker of miracles, forgiver of sins.

That whoever believes in him

Kingdom evangelism has an awareness of where it comes from, seeking to honour its past roots, as well as aim clearly for its target with a sense of future destiny. For the Jews there was never any secular/spiritual split (a Greek concept exemplified by the heretical Gnostics and also to some extent by the Stoics). All of life was about God. So, belief for the Jew wasn't about adopting a head-based system of beliefs, ideals, precepts, principles and philosophies, like Alice in Wonderland struggling to 'believe six impossible things before breakfast'! Rather, belief for the Jew meant a lifestyle-based, wholehearted commitment of mind, feelings and will. It was more about relationship and trust than legalistic, ritualistic dogma. When it did degenerate into legalism the Jews lost the heart of what they believed. So, kingdom evangelism, operating under God's grace not law, stresses relationship with Jesus first, based on commitment and trust, and sees doctrine as vital, but as a mean to an end (that is, read the Bible to reveal Jesus, not to become bibliolotrous), not as an end in itself. Truth cannot be separated from Jesus (Jn 14:6), and though unchanging, truth *is* multi-faceted. To quote Jim Wallis, 'What you *do* on Monday morning is what you believe. Everything else is religion.' Or have another look at James 1:22–25.

Shall not perish

You don't have to persuade many people of the reality of hell— a lot of them are living there already. Perishing can be a process that starts before you die, and hell (never designed for people anyway, but for Satan and the like—Mt 25:41) is the final stage.

Kingdom evangelism recognises that Jesus not only saved us from hell, but also from perishing here and now. His salvation (*sozo*) equates with forgiveness, wholeness, healing, restoration, reconciliation and peace (it is the New Testament version of the Hebrew Old Testament word *shalom*). Peace is where our will has ceased to oppose the perfect, good and pleasing will of God (Rom 12:1–2) and we have become daily living sacrifices.

But have eternal life

So, kingdom evangelism isn't just about being saved *from* something, but being saved *to* something. And just as hell for some starts now, so too for God's children, heaven starts now. Eternal life isn't just quantitative (ie, goes on for ever and ever, and what are we going to do for all that time?). It is also qualitative, hence Jesus' promise in John 10:10. In our current world order and spirit of the age, kingdom evangelism replaces communism with Christian hope; liberalism with Christian faith; humanism with Christian love; and materialism with Christian worship.

ABC of doing it

When it comes to applying all of the above to the church diary, how practical can we be? Kingdom evangelism will be based on the conviction that though not all are called to be evangelists (Eph 4:11–13), all *are* called to be witnesses (Mt 28:16–20). Therefore, strategic church evangelism will seek to:

1. *Identify* the key people who are evangelists (Fuller Theological Seminary church growth studies indicate about 10% of any congregation).

2. *Train and motivate* the body to the works of service—in this case evangelism.

3. *Facilitate structures* which will enable relevant evangelism from the whole church.

Training

The best people to identify evangelists *are* evangelists. This is why kingdom evangelism often avails itself of ministries (built on relationships) from outside the local situation. It is all too easy to 'sit' on people for their past mistakes, especially young people, and develop 'people blindness' to those nearest us in our own congregations. When key individuals are identified, they are candidates for specific input and training in personal evangelism, preaching, public speaking and youth communication. (Having learned to communicate with young people, for example in schools, you can communicate across the age range. Something which is *not* true if you only learn to communicate with adults.) Also, training is needed in setting and reaching faith targets, in time management and in spiritual gifts. These are the people to put in charge of your church's evangelism programme. These are God's 'breakthrough' people.

This training can be through workshop programmes such as covering the basics of the theology of evangelism; Who does it? To whom? Why? What stops us?; how to witness effectively; communication techniques; leading someone to Christ; using our story (testimony); whose territory do we fight on? and spiritual warfare.

The trained team should then be aimed at a specific strategy, as carefully planned to service your area and your community as your church spending would be! Kingdom evangelism at its best is a combination of 'events evangelism', working off the back of ongoing 'friendship evangelism'. It is *not* one or the other. The church's strategy in evangelism should, I suggest, involve specific dates/events/personnel/finances for the following, subsequent to training:

Door-to-door leafleting and visiting
Consistent streetwork
Schools and colleges work
Regular guest meetings
Action house groups (which are evangelistic and not pastoral)

In addition there could be special events like:

Pub events
Restaurant takeovers
Cabarets and supper clubs
Leisure centre hiring
'It's a Knockout' days
Folk evenings
Youth centre work
Prison events
Involvement in 'secular' events, such as carnivals, fêtes, fun days, galas, processions and charities
Occasional mission weeks in schools or on council estates
Ongoing social action (local hospices, hospital radio, old age pensioners' homes, hospitals, ACET [Aids Care and Education Training] schemes, etc)

In our own church we found that an evangelism team, far from 'doing it all', is a good structure to aid the church to do kingdom evangelism. It is made up of hand-picked, carefully trained church folk, with a heart for expanding the kingdom and a willingness to make mistakes!

Two final pleas

First, that evangelists, for so long pushed out on their own from churches because of their activist nature and their often headstrong and insecure character, are welcomed back into the body centrally. Yes, they disturb the status quo. Yes, they will ask awkward questions about structures and religion and introversion. But no, they shouldn't be allowed to be lone wolves, highly individualistic and unaccountable. Instead, they should, at leadership level (elders, deacons, PCCs), have input to the direction of your church. The real biblical evangelist can be tested on two fronts: does he/she consistently see conversions? And is he/she able to enthuse, motivate, train and work within the local church, to enable effective witness?

Secondly, a plea that kingdom evangelism is allowed to complement the whole church in its modelling of the kingdom, and so isn't at war with the pastoral ministry, as is often intimated in evangelical circles. Kingdom evangelism will have as its goal the Colossians 1:28 mandate (and also Matthew 28:16–20) to present people whole/perfect (*teleos*) in Christ; to make disciples and not to manipulate decisions. We must therefore have an eye to the proper integration of new believers. Kingdom evangelism *cannot* be tacked on to existing church structures. It will be a radical challenge to *all* of them (outreach, nurture, youth work, Bible study and prayer meetings, praise and worship, prophecy, etc). This will necessitate flexible structures; a rolling (on/off) programme of nurture and discipleship, where foundations are laid concerning the Christian faith and the Christian local church. At our own church, Revelation Chichester/Bognor Regis, we constantly run at least one (currently three) fifteen-week foundation courses for new Christians. The courses run each week—on housegroup nights to establish the pattern—and are run by trained leaders with pastoral helpers. They are based on friendship, and not just on doctrine; on lifestyle and personal ministry, and not just on dogma and words. Pioneer will shortly publish the course we have written, and the Pioneer Bible Study Booklets could be used one to one. But, whatever is used, training, planning and fellowship are *key* if kingdom evangelism is to produce long-term kingdom citizens.

I have tried to include in this chapter a mixture of the general and the specific, so that you can catch a little of my vision and my understanding of kingdom evangelism. Enough, I hope, to be spiritually practical and practically spiritual. I am mindful of two of God's warnings: 'My people are destroyed from lack of knowledge' (Hos 4:6), and, 'Where there is no revelation, the people cast off restraint' (Prov 29:18). I hope there is enough here both to stimulate your mind with knowledge and your heart with revelation towards kingdom evangelism, because there is little which is more fun, more frustrating and more exciting!

11

Releasing the Supernatural in the Local Church

Martin Scott

Martin Scott led the Pioneer People, Cobham for several years, before working in the Pioneer South and West of London region, having input into churches particularly at a faith and vision level. He is also in growing demand as a speaker alongside his healing ministry. Martin is married to Sue and they have two young children, Benjamin and Judith.

She explained to the preacher that just a few minutes earlier quite miraculously God had healed her. She had come to the meeting with an enormous growth on her stomach which made her appear nine months pregnant. Over the course of two months she had gained 28 lbs in weight. Now she stood there to proclaim that the growth had instantly and totally disappeared. As the meeting progressed I watched as the deaf heard and the cripple walked— the Spirit of God was present to heal in an indisputable way. I sat and watched, with my heart filled with excitement and my eyes wet with tears. How good and powerful God is. We were not in Africa or some faith-filled third world country. This was Britain. Oh yes, the preacher was from the USA, but it was happening to ordinary, common-sense British people.

Stories of that nature could be repeated from many areas of the world today. I was recently in an informal meeting where a church leader began to recount how a young lady from his church had moved over to Paris to work among her own racial group. She experienced considerable success—some responded to Christ and soon a church was established. During her time in Paris she received phone calls from Switzerland, one of which was for her to pray for a deaf boy. She prayed over the telephone, and as a result the boy could hear. God had totally healed him. As a result of this and other healings she was asked to fly to Switzerland to explain the Christian way of salvation to this group of Hindus who had made the telephone calls. They were now confessing that her God—the Christian God—is the one who has the power to answer prayer.

How do we respond to these stories of the miraculous? We might try to explain them under a theology of the sovereignty of God—he sovereignly chooses to heal some Tamil boys in Switzerland, but he chooses not to do that in our church. Or we might be sceptical of the reports we hear. Perhaps we even allow cynicism to rise up through an attitude of superiority. What would be a good and honest response? I would like to suggest that we do not go running after signs and wonders for their own sake, but that we allow the Holy Spirit to plant a godly desire in our hearts— a longing that our churches might demonstrate the same dynamic Christianity we read about in the Book of Acts.

The genuine article?

A number of years ago I was reading the guarantee on the back of a chocolate bar. My mind wandered and I thought that if God had attached a guarantee to the Christianity we had received in the West it might go something like this: 'We want you to enjoy Christianity at its best, just as it left the empty grave. If, after 2,000 years, it is damaged in any way and you are not entirely satisfied with it, please return the complete package saying where and when it was purchased. We will be glad to replace it with the genuine article.'

I do believe the product we have today is deficient in certain aspects. This is most certainly true in the area of signs and wonders. I would advocate that now is the time for the British church to look again at the New Testament and see what the Bible teaches about the supernatural so that our expectations can be founded both in Scripture and reality.

I am a convinced charismatic. I believe in the outpouring of the Holy Spirit and the exercise of the gifts of the Holy Spirit. I have been thrilled to be involved in what has been termed the 'charismatic movement'. However, I also believe that we are yet to see a greater manifestation of his power in and through the church. Over recent years there has been an increased interest in the subject of the miraculous. One has only to read the list of new books coming onto the Christian market, or to attend some of the popular seminars on the subject to see that it is one of the major topics of the moment. Great steps forward have been taken in recent years to see signs and wonders restored to their rightful place within the body of Christ, yet I am convinced that we have only just begun to see what is on God's heart in this area.

Need for the supernatural

I believe the supernatural is vital if we are going to break out of a purely middle-class environment. Apathy and materialism are dominating forces in so many lives today. It is the supernatural that will help us to cut through this. God is alive and he wants to confront every other false god—whether the pagan gods of the heathen or the sophisticated Western gods of materialism and science. We will need the supernatural dimension if we are going to see more than cerebral converts and begin to produce convinced disciples (Rom 15:18).

The miraculous is an integral part of the gospel that we proclaim. We could summarise Jesus' instructions to his disciples as follows: 'Proclaim that there is another King and then show evidence that he has taken up his reign. This evidence is to include healing the sick, casting out demons, cleansing the lepers, and raising the dead!' By that point of the 'presentation' most of the hearers would have been convinced that Jesus was a viable King.

Jesus gave us no mandate to change his commission—in fact he said that this gospel of the kingdom is to be taken to every nation before the end is to come. It would also seem that he did not expect people to believe the gospel message without the confirming signs. To believe that this commission and challenge might still be directed towards us as believers probably does not sit comfortably with us. We are quite aware of how far short of that ideal (or norm?) we come.

The early disciples preached the kingdom rule of God and he in turn confirmed the message to the unbeliever with signs. The emphasis on the kingdom of God in recent years has paved the way for a fresh move of God that will include the miraculous. If we are to see our words authenticated in the same way as Jesus and the early disciples did, we know there must yet be a greater manifestation of power to come. Here we experience the tension of living in the overlap of two ages. The kingdom of God is a present reality, but it has not yet come in its glorious completeness. We must press forward to see more and more of the kingdom reality displayed in the here and now.

Anyone wanting to move in the supernatural power of the kingdom would love to have a testimony similar to that of Paul's experience on Malta in Acts 28. All the sick on the island were brought to him and were healed. However, we need to start where we are. Like the athlete we need to begin to run the race, not just wistfully dream of standing on the winner's podium.

A learning environment

If we are looking for these gifts to flourish within our churches, then we need to be creating a suitable environment where they can develop. There needs to be an environment where people can exercise the gifts and run the risk of getting it wrong. Before we insist on decency and order, we need to have something to bring decency and order to. 'Let all things be done' is the first injunction— 'decently and in order' is the second. If we are so preoccupied with getting everything in order that we never do anything, we will be in danger of quenching any spirit of faith that might be present.

We do obviously need to be sensitive and wise. We do not want the gifts of the Holy Spirit to be abused by encouraging the making of mistakes, but unless we create an environment for experiment, we are unlikely to move forward very quickly.

The manifestations of the Holy Spirit are here to fulfil for us the same role that they did for Jesus—they are to demonstrate the age to come within this present age in a practical and visible way. Jesus cast out demons and then declared that the kingdom of God was present through that manifestation of the Holy Spirit. We have a great need to make the coming kingdom visible to people both in and outside of our churches. It is for this reason we need to move forward. Jesus himself said that Sodom would have repented if it had seen the miraculous power he had demonstrated in cities like Capernaum (Mt 11:23).

The challenge before us is to begin to see the sick healed and so help our communities to grow in faith in order that we can begin to see even greater miracles take place. It would seem from the record of Jesus in Nazareth that even he needed to work with a community in faith in order to see great miracles take place, although he could still 'lay his hands on a few sick people and heal them' (Mk 6:5; see also Mt 13:57–58).

Leaders must set the agenda

In Acts 19:11 Luke records that Paul saw extraordinary miracles, but until leaders today take a serious look at the whole issue of the miraculous, I am not convinced that we will even see ordinary miracles in our churches.

If we are in leadership we need to realise that it is our responsibility to set the agenda under God. The supernatural has such prominence within the New Testament that although not every leader will have the burden to activate such things themselves, leadership must set the direction and place the supernatural on their agendas if our churches are going to sit within the tradition of New Testament Christianity.

In order to do this we need to implement whatever education programme is necessary, and as far as the supernatural is concerned education needs to be both didactic and practical. I would suggest that the most suitable forum for this is that of the seminar or workshop. Teaching from the Scriptures can be followed by discussion and the practical implementation of the gifts of the Holy Spirit.

It is vital that we give teaching on the subject of the supernatural. Nothing comes automatically. Many churches are built on the foundation of firm friendships and relationships. This does not happen automatically but takes place over a period of months and years as consistent teaching is given on the nature of church and the centrality of relationships to church life. Similarly, the supernatural will not occur overnight. A firm foundation is prepared through consistent teaching.

We also need to expose ourselves and our churches to people of proven supernatural ministry. We are not to set such people on a pedestal, but we do need to realise that Jesus' method was both didactic and practical. We can invite such people into our churches to teach and to demonstrate.

Stepping out

After creating forums where teaching and practice can take place, we then need to move towards giving the Holy Spirit a suitable platform where he can move and demonstrate himself in the public arena. This will mean taking the plunge and moving from the theory to where we actually 'lay our hands on the sick' in whichever way is appropriate for our situation.

In our home church we have run workshops on prophecy and on healing. Five years ago we knew that we had to take the plunge and go public and allow God to move outside of our safe environment. Since then we have held regular healing meetings aimed particularly at those who are not Christians. The first few meetings were nerve-racking. We certainly did not see the dead raised, but as we stepped out in faithfulness to God we proved that he was with us. God healed some people in our very first public meeting, which was a great thrill, and as we have gone on the evidence of God's power being present has become greater.

We have also seen salvation come to people in those meetings because they have seen and heard the good news. Recently we had one young man come along who was sceptical, but God touched him significantly with his power. As he lay on the floor under the power of the Holy Spirit he had something to think about. Later he talked with a leader who spoke by the word of knowledge into his life. He was no longer sceptical and was ready to follow Jesus for himself. We might have a long way to go, but at least we have made a start.

Sometimes I feel it might be easier to have an itinerant ministry where praying for the sick is concerned, but we need to see that Jesus is committed to seeing the supernatural released within our communities in order that we can be effective witnesses where we are.

A lesson from Abraham

The first account of healing in Scripture is that of Abraham praying for the household of Abimelech in order that the women might conceive. At first sight this is not too dramatic—but what about Abraham's own personal experience? How would we feel praying for someone else to receive something which we had not yet received ourselves? By this stage Abraham was an old man and Sarah remained barren in spite of God's promise. Here he was required to pray for a number of women who were also barren. He faced the choice: would he live within his experience, or would he step out in obedience to what he believed God was asking him? Would he say, 'It doesn't work,' or would he go for it? Abraham was bold enough not to compromise God's word by restricting it to his own experience. The results were impressive: 'God healed Abimelech, his wife and his slave girls so they could have children again' (Gen 20:17). Two verses later we read, 'And the Lord did for Sarah what he had promised' (Gen 21:1).

I am sure that the answer to his own personal situation was tied both to his continuous obedience to God and to his faith. He refused to allow himself to be limited by his own personal experience. Little wonder Paul calls him the father of the faith. It is this same spirit of faith which we will need if we are to see God fulfil his word in our day and generation. Paul embodied this sort of fighting faith when he declared that 'we might be knocked down but we are never knocked out' (2 Cor 4:9, J B PHILLIPS).

There is often a gap between our experience and the teaching of Scripture, and we therefore need to have a curriculum which will help us see the gap closed and a spirit of faith and boldness which will cause us to pursue God.

What if it does not work?

Perhaps we ought to ask, 'What if it does work?' So often we are programmed to expect the negative. If it does not work then the short answer is, 'Try, try again.'

We will have to deal with our propensity to being afraid of failure. It is far better we obey, and learn through our mistakes and failures. We will have failures and disappointments, but it is important that we do not compromise what God has said to us over the issue of the supernatural.

We do need to get on and exercise our faith in God in the area of the supernatural. Practice might not make us perfect, but it should help us in our quest to close the gap between our experience and the teaching of the New Testament. There will be disappointments, there will be unanswered questions. But if we are obedient and press through those disappointments, there will also be great joy as we increasingly see God heal people through our ministry or church.

What about those who are not Christians?

Many people are afraid to pray with those who are not Christians because of the fear of nothing happening. We need to deal with the fear and be obedient to God when he prompts us in this direction. We do not want to act in presumption and bring dishonour to Jesus' name, but perhaps it is equally true that we also need to deal with the problem of presuming God will not heal them through us.

Our experience would suggest that God is very willing to heal those who are not Christians. We have found that this is particularly true among the younger generation who are honestly searching for reality. We are not here to 'put God in a corner', but we are here to help honest seekers find a living God.

Even when it does not 'work', I believe we will have shown the love and compassion of Jesus to that person, and through the laying-on of hands they will have 'seen' something of the unseen realm. Let us not be foolish, but let us not hold back unduly either.

Parting thoughts to those who feel called to pursue a supernatural ministry

1. Be convinced with regard to your beliefs over the teaching of Scripture. Healing ministries differ over their interpretation of Scripture passages, but they are individually convinced in their own minds. I believe God honours them because they have searched the Scriptures and act upon their own personal convictions. You will need your own convictions, not the second-hand views of someone else. Find out what you believe God has to say on the issue and then decide to develop your hope and faith in God's word until you begin to see the gap closed between your experience and your theology. Do not compromise and base your theology on your experience.

2. There can be no real progress in God without an accompanying heart-cry for help, revelation and wisdom. Genuine prayer (and I would suggest also fasting) will be necessary for you to progress in the supernatural. Pray and fast in response to God. Do not do it in order to earn merit with him. We need to realise that no area of Christianity is based on performance. Success will not come through sacrifice (the sacrifice of Jesus is sufficient for

all time), but through learning in everyday situations an obedience to Jesus.

3. Give yourself the opportunity of being exposed to other healing ministries. You might not like everything you see, but it will be a means of encouragement and learning.

4. Finally, continually fix your eyes on Jesus who is the author and finisher of our faith. 'Yet at present we do not see everything subject to him [mankind]. But we see Jesus, who was made a little lower than the angels, now crowned with glory and honour because he suffered death, so that by the grace of God he might taste death for everyone' (Heb 2:8–9).

The historic Jesus has conquered the devil and destroyed all his works and is now seated at the right hand of God. We are seated there with him and I am convinced that as we open up our hearts to see this Jesus our faith will rise and our experience will begin to resemble New Testament theology.

I do believe we have a rich heritage of relationships. It is for this reason that I have a great deal of hope that God can do something special with us in the area of signs and wonders. The joy of knowing that we are working with Jesus and seeing a little more of the kingdom of God come to this earth will help us to cope with our disappointments and our successes. It will be well worth the effort, time and dedication that are given to God in our pursuit of seeing the supernatural released in local churches.

12

Music and Worship

Noel Richards

Noel Richards is a well-known songwriter and worship leader. His worship album By Your Side *has received high acclaim in several parts of the world. Noel is married to Tricia and they have two children, Sam and Amy, with 'lodger Steph' and 'Barney the dog'. He is also the author of* The Worshipping Church *in the Pioneer Perspective series (Word (UK) 1992).*

Our primary role as believers is to be worshippers, and music has a vital role to play in this. Let's beware, then, of making the mistake of seeing this as a specialist subject, appealing only to the musicians and worship leaders.

The power of music and song

I believe Martin Luther was on the right track when he wrote: 'Next to theology, I give music the highest place and honour. Music is the art of the prophets, the only art that can calm the agitations of the soul; it is one of the most magnificent and delightful presents God has given us.'

God created music for our pleasure and for his pleasure. He likes music! The Bible is full of references to music and song. In Job 38:7 we see the morning stars singing together at the dawn of creation. Zephaniah 3:17 speaks of God rejoicing over us with singing. The Old Testament prophets often sang their prophecies and there are many biblical passages which would have been sung. Jesus descended from the line of David, who was a great musician, songwriter and worshipper.

Truth is often best communicated in a song. In Deuteronomy 31:19 we see God giving Moses a song to teach the sons of Israel, to put it on their lips. Colossians 3:16 tells us to teach and admonish one another with psalms, hymns and spiritual songs. How did we first learn the alphabet? Most of us will remember the tune that accompanies A, B, C, D, etc. When I was in Sunday school, we had a song which enabled us to memorise the books of the Bible.

Music and song are a major means of influencing the masses. Somebody once said, 'Let me write the songs of a nation . . . I don't care who writes its laws.' Songs stay in the heart together with the philosophy and ideology behind the lyrics. In America during the Vietnam War era, the song 'Give peace a chance' was the anthem of the anti-war protesters.

Music brings healing and deliverance. We see a powerful example of this in the story of Saul being tormented by an evil spirit. His servants knew the power of music to bring relief in this situation. David was summoned and as this anointed musician played, the evil spirit would depart from Saul and he would feel better (1 Sam 16:14–23).

Music can be a prayer to the Lord. He gave Moses a promise in Numbers 10:9 that when they went into battle and sounded their trumpets, he would remember them and rescue them from their enemies. Habakkuk 3 is a prayer in musical form.

Music can stir up the prophetic gifts. In 1 Samuel 10:5 Saul was told about a procession of prophets who were prophesying accompanied by music. In 1 Chronicles 25:1 David set apart those who would prophesy accompanied by music. In my own worship team, I have individuals who have a prophetic singing gift. They find themselves being stirred to prophesy and do so while being accompanied by the musicians.

Music is vital in worship. We see music playing this important role throughout the whole of Scripture. Indeed, the Book of Psalms expresses to the Lord the whole range of human emotions. Music and song are seen throughout the history of the church as being a means of expressing praise and worship to God.

God's taste in music

What sort of music does God like? I believe God likes all the different styles of music, from gentle to loud, from classical to heavy metal and everything in between. There is no such thing as 'Christian' music. Music is music. It is neither good nor bad; it is neutral. What man does with music makes it either good or evil. I believe it is possible for Christians to play any style of music and glorify God in it.

Satan has distorted every gift that God gave us, and music is no exception. His influence has pervaded every style of music. Many of the 'great' classical composers lived lives of debauchery and died of alcoholism or some sexual disease. Some of them were stark raving mad! Yet many Christians have classical music in their record collection. We must redeem all the musical cultures, taking from Satan what rightfully belongs to us.

We know we are getting old when we listen to the pop music our children like and find we have no appreciation of it. We think it all sounds the same and we cannot hear the words! We feel threatened by it in the same way that previous generations of parents were threatened by The Beatles or The Rolling Stones. Often we as Christians brand as 'demonic' what we do not understand or what we feel threatened by.

My cultural preference is for rock music and I feel happiest when worshipping God and expressing my faith in that particular style. Others are more into 'rapping' or dance music, and they write songs of worship in that genre. Some Christian bands play heavy metal and reach the followers of that kind of music with the gospel. The American band Stryper are renowned for throwing Bibles into the audience at their concerts.

I would like to see Christians getting involved in the music industry and breaking into the pop world. It would be wonderful to see Christians leading the way and setting the trends, being the role models for today's youth.

Music is important

It is encouraging to see both music and musicians being given a place of importance in the church these days. Much of the worship has moved on from the 'hymn–prayer–hymn' sandwich. Musicians are playing more creatively, with the Scriptures being sung or read to musical accompaniment and room being given to prophetic singing and much more.

I have been in meetings where the musicians have played from beginning to end, accompanying worship, prayer, Scripture reading and amplifying the teaching. This of course calls for more than your standard church organist playing the hymns!

We are now seeing the need for a greater range of instruments. Keyboards, strings, woodwinds, brass, percussion—all are finding their way into the worship bands today. This is giving us so much more scope in our worship. Recently, I was at a large celebration where a fifty-piece orchestra led the people in worship. It was powerful!

There was a time not long ago when Christians regarded drums as being evil! However, percussion and rhythm belong to God. After all, he created rhythm. Psalm 150 speaks of resounding cymbals being used in praise.

Qualities in musicians

I look for two qualities in the musicians I work with. They are *gift* and *character*.

I want to work with musicians who are gifted musically and in sensitivity to the Holy Spirit, as we read in 1 Chronicles 25:1–7.

With regard to character, these musicians need to be people who are faithful and reliable. Individuals who have a servant heart. I also look for musicians who are worshippers and pursue a lifestyle of worship. To me, character is of prime importance. I would rather work with a less gifted musician who has allowed God to mould his/her character than a brilliant one who has not.

In our churches we should be grooming young individuals for a future ministry in music. We do not want the same people leading the music and worship for ever and ever. If children aged twelve years and under decide to be top athletes by the time they are seventeen or eighteen, and succeed like some of the Wimbledon tennis champions, why can't we do that in the church? We may have children in our churches who will be the worship leaders and songwriters of the future. Let's release them to go for all that they want to be for God.

Music—prophetic or nostalgic?

David Pawson said:

> One of the first signs that God is moving anywhere is music. God is very musical, therefore whenever God is moving in a new way there is a burst of new music. . . . The tragedy is that music is also the last thing to disappear after God has stopped moving and then music, instead of being prophetic, becomes nostalgic and people sing the 'good old hymns'. Their hearts go backwards while God is moving forward.

Every fresh move of God has brought a new wave of music and song and affected the church's worship. The traditional hymns by the likes of Wesley were radical and prophetic when first written. They were the popular songs of the day. The fact that they have stood the test of time and are still relevant today, is a mark of their quality. Will today's new worship songs still be sung in 200 years' time?

Many of today's traditional hymns and songs were frowned upon when first written because they used the popular 'worldly' music of the time. However, they became acceptable and were absorbed into the worship services of the denominational churches. But the church was never meant to stand still musically and sing only the 'good old hymns', year in year out. God is a creative being, who is constantly bringing fresh direction to his people, together with new songs that convey and express what is happening. Sadly, the name a church has over its door, together with the songs it sings, gives you an idea of where the revelation stopped and it chose to settle.

The challenge to us is whether or not we will continue to move forward and release new songs and music that have a prophetic edge, or settle for nostalgia.

A good worship leader will incorporate old and new songs into his/her repertoire (see Matthew 13:52).

Songwriters need to 'sit at the feet' of the prophets and distil their revelation into songs that will put God's 'now' word onto people's lips. Songs such as 'Bind us together' took a prophetic word from God to the far corners of the globe. Such is the power of music and song.

I am excited by the current crop of songs that is sweeping through our churches. However, they do tend to be middle-of-the-road from a musical point of view. The strength of this is that they do appeal to a wide constituency. The downside of this is that they often lag behind contemporary music. We need to see songs written that are bang up to date musically and which set the musical trends instead of following them.

A lifestyle of worship

We should not be switching into worship mode when we go to a church meeting. Worship is for life, not just for meetings. The quality of the worship we experience in our churches is a direct result of the quality of the worshippers. Corporate worship is a reflection of individual worship. As a worship leader, I cannot motivate people to worship if they are not worshippers. God wants us to develop a lifestyle of worship where we see the whole of our life as being worship, and not simply the songs we sing on a Sunday morning. God does not want us to have a compartmentalised approach to living. He wants to be involved in all aspects of our life.

These are some of the areas of our lifestyles that affect the credibility of our worship:

Relationships

It is vital that we have a right relationship with our brothers and sisters. It is difficult to bless God when we are in conflict with a fellow believer. The fragrance of worship is soured by disunity (Mt 5:23–24). God commands blessing on those who dwell in unity (Ps 133:1–3).

Speech

Our words are powerful. We can never take them back once they have been uttered (I guess we all wish we could at one time or another). Words can be creative or destructive. How can we be slandering someone one moment and then trying to bless God the next? It is totally incongruous (Jas 3:9–12).

Actions

Sin is no longer an inevitability because we have been regenerated and empowered by the Holy Spirit. There may be times though when we find sin has crept in through the back door, for whatever reason. It is then that we either choose to confess or cover up. If we confess to God and to one another, light comes into our lives. We do not fear being found out and the issue is dealt with. Our relationship with God is restored and worship can flow.

Obedience

In 1 Samuel 15, Saul was instructed to destroy the Amalekites and all they had. Saul disobeyed the Lord and spared their king and kept the best sheep and cattle. When confronted by Samuel, Saul lied, saying that God's command had been obeyed. 'What then is this bleating of sheep in my ears?' asked Samuel. Saul's excuse was that he intended to sacrifice the animals to the Lord. 'To obey is better than to sacrifice,' declared Samuel.

The sound of the 'bleating sheep' of disobedience will drown out the sound of our worship.

Heart attitude

Are our hearts filled with gratitude towards the Lord? Are we generous towards him and others? Do we give him the best, or does he take second place in our affections? Is there any cynicism that robs God, others and ourselves of blessing? Are we proud, or walking in humility? Do we desire to serve, or do we seek leadership for our own gain?

The sincerity of our hearts is what God looks at when we worship him. He sees beyond the songs and outward appearance we present.

Praise God continually

Wherever we are and whatever we are doing, we can offer up praise and thanksgiving to the Lord. The communication channels are always open. We can experience his presence in every circumstance of life (Heb 13:15).

What are we meeting for?

Each time we come together in our congregation, this must be our question. What does God want from our event? How does he want us to worship him? There are times when all we will do in a meeting is worship the Lord. On other occasions, we may sing just one song and that will be appropriate. At other times, we may not worship at all. Why does every meeting have to start with a time of worship? Why not get the speaker on first and maybe worship at the end of the meeting? To revere the Lord is to do what he wants. Let's make sure we are doing this, or we may find that our worship is simply self-indulgent cultural enjoyment.

To have a good time of worship means that we give to God what he wants. We worship him in the way that he wants us to and not in a way which simply satisfies us. To bless the Lord means quite literally to give God a good time. Our times of worship are to do with what he gets out of it, not what we get out of it. Any blessing we get from worshipping the Lord is a bonus. We worship him because he alone is worthy of our adoration. In whatever circumstances we find ourselves, we can always worship God because he does not change.

Be flexible in worship

The programme of songs, prayers, Scripture readings, etc, is simply scaffolding on which our worship is built. Scaffolding is known as 'temporary works'. It is there to facilitate the building programme, not to hinder it. Unfortunately, the 'scaffolding' of our Sunday morning worship can remain the same for years on end. It becomes cherished, and to suggest changing it is tantamount to heresy. It runs like clockwork, and like a good Swiss watch always keeps to time. It has to, because Sunday lunch is more important than a visitation of the Holy Spirit. In fact he does not need to show up because the well-organised 'order of service' runs well enough without him. Indeed, if he did turn up the 'order of service' would become the 'dis-order of service'! He does not make for tidy meetings. However, we cannot ask the Holy Spirit to honour our meetings with his presence and then dictate to him how we want him to behave.

Our worship must be the kind that is controlled by the Holy Spirit so that we can give God what he desires and deserves. Anything less is just a lot of noise and pointless activity.

13
Good News for Little Angels

Ishmael

Ishmael (real name Ian Smale) is Director of the Glorie Company, which is a ministry to families. He is best known for his 'Glories and Miseries' albums, books and praise parties. He is in much demand in the UK and overseas in encouraging family worship, meetings and the involvement of children in church life. He has authored several successful books, including an autobiography and novels. Ishmael is married to Irene and they have three children. This chapter is reproduced by permission from his book Angels with Dirty Faces *(Kingsway 1989).*

'Please Mummy, don't make me go to that noisy Glorie Company,' screams an insecure little nine-year-old who is making as much fuss as a vegetarian forced to enter a steak house. 'But you must go to Ishmael's meeting. You'll be able to learn all about Jesus and how to become a Christian, and anyway, Daddy and I have to go to our meeting so you can't stay with us.'

This is quite a common occurrence, and of course some children are frightened on their first visit to a hall packed with hundreds of other excitable children whom they don't know. I'm sure *I* would be—wouldn't you?

It doesn't help for the child to discover that another reason they must go and be with Ishmael is because the parents couldn't get another babysitter to look after them and Ishmael is a good babysitter who also teaches stories from the Bible. But it goes further. There are so many times when I have found myself in a situation in which I just cannot win. 'I'm sorry, Madam, but I cannot teach your child all about Jesus and salvation in the next hour. It will take your child that long to settle down and not feel scared, insecure and threatened, and it will take me that long to learn your child's name. But as I do preach on believing for the miraculous and achieving the impossible I will do my best. . . .'

Then come the 'divine' requests which instead of being taken to the Lord, are brought to me. 'I believe that the Lord is going to use you tonight to save my child,' says one, and, 'I know mine will speak in tongues for the first time,' says another, and, 'God is going to anoint you to heal my son's deaf ear tonight,' pipes up a third, and from that moment on comes the flow of great expectations. It's all very flattering, but I know that if I allow that sort of pressure to get to me, I will end up praying for everything and seeing nothing happen. To try and get people to see that they must look to God and not to human beings seems almost as impossible as the miracle they are after.

Don't get me wrong; I love to see parents with great vision for their children. But I wish they could realise that I, like many others, am just a Spirit-filled Christian, and they have the same, or possibly more, access to the Holy Spirit, especially when their prayers involve their own children. So much more could be done in the home, if only they could believe and understand that.

I am convinced that children can become believers at a very early age. I know that some critics would question exactly how much children can understand, but my argument is: how much does any-one of any age really understand when they first become a believer?

I try to picture Mr Average, who almost certainly, if he lives in Britain, no longer comes from a Christian country. The chances are that except for the odd christening, wedding or funeral he has never darkened the door of a darkened building known to him as a church. As far as Christian teaching goes, all he remembers are a few well-diluted Bible verses delivered by an agnostic head-master from his primary school assembly days. And his experience of worship is the odd Sunday evening in front of the telly, accidentally tuning in to the wrong channel and ending up watching a few minutes of *Songs of Praise* instead of the programme he was intending to see.

It is a similar process of learning and being re-educated for him as it is for a child. In fact it will probably be easier for the child because he will not have lived as long on this planet, and although he has sinned, he has not had the time to be so tainted by the wickedness around him, or to develop the confusion and doubts that adults discover come quite naturally with age.

Yes, children are much more open to being taught, as they, unlike many of their forebears, realise that they don't have all the answers to life's problems. All they have inherited are the unanswered questions.

I am thankful to the Lord that the great news of new birth and new life is simple. Some of our evangelists, however, would obviously disagree with me. Having heard some of their so-called simple expositions of 'salvation', I'd say that there was a lot more chance of a camel going sideways through the eye of a needle than any normal pagan understanding a word of what was said.

Thankfully for the unsaved, the words of the Holy Spirit, whose voice they are really hearing, is a lot clearer, more direct, precise and easier to comprehend than most evangelists will ever be. I am sure that at almost any age people can understand what we call the 'ABC of Salvation', and as in the Bible we are all called to share our faith with others, I am convinced that we do not need a degree in theology to tell people how to give their lives back to God.

It is a sad indictment on our church system that both adults and children are being taught how they ought to invite unbelievers along to a 'meeting', rather than being taught how to invite them to know the Lord Jesus. We need to teach both young and old how to pray with their friends and to see them saved, and that this is not just the job of the church leader when he gives his Sunday evening appeal.

Although the Holy Spirit will lead individuals to pray in different ways, let me give you some guidelines on how I personally would pray for children, which may be of some help.

Please bear with me as I run through a few details that I believe to be important for the children to have some knowledge of if they are to understand the basics of becoming a Christian. May I also add that it is not just the words you say, but the sincerity and simplicity in the way you communicate this message that is going to help the children understand and respond. Obviously the following is a more detailed guide for reference for the older reader. When passing it on to a child, one would need to use even simpler words and expressions. And remember that while *we* are doing the evangelising, it is going to be the Holy Spirit who does the saving.

Here we go then. Imagine we are face to face with a child or a crowd of children asking how to become a Christian.

First, I am a keen believer in teaching the theology of the Trinity. I believe that God, from the beginning to the end of time, exists in three persons: God the Father, God the Son and God the Holy Spirit. Although it is hard for our finite minds to understand, these three persons are not just three separate 'parts' of God; each of the persons is God.

Now, although the Father, Son and Holy Spirit do have different roles to play, they are all involved in bringing about the brand new life of the born-again Christian. So right from the word go, I teach the person I am sharing the good news with just a little bit of how the three persons of the Trinity are involved.

Although some may think that this would sound confusing to children at such an early stage, I have found it to be a lot less confusing than when later on they hear people singing about and praying to various members of the Trinity and our poor young baby Christian hasn't got a clue about what or to whom the people are praying.

Father God

I make it clear that the Bible teaches us that we have all sinned (done things that have hurt God) and fallen short of Father God's glory (not been the kind of people he created us to be).

So that they don't suspect I am making things up, I find it a good idea to show them Romans 3:23. They can then see this is what the Bible teaches. (Please make sure you use a modern translation so that they can understand it.)

I then explain that doing wrong comes naturally, and doing right demands effort. Even if right from when they were tiny no one had taught them to do wrong things, no one needed to; it was one of the few things they were immediately good at. I remind them that it was not their mums and dads who taught them to do wrong; in fact, most mums and dads spend most of their time struggling to teach them to do right.

I have never had to spend long convincing a child that he is not perfect. Nowadays I have more trouble trying to teach a child self-worth. Let me emphasise that no one has forced them to do wrong actions, have wrong thoughts and say wrong things; they have in fact consciously or subconsciously chosen to do these things for themselves.

Do they realise how it breaks Father God's heart when we choose to do things that, deep down, we know upset him? I then ask the child to say sorry for the things that come to mind, and if he can think of one specific thing he continually does that upsets Father God, he should not only say sorry for this, but should ask God to give him the strength to stop doing that thing completely.

Although I may not use such a long word as 'repentance', that is what I know God wants to see: a complete change of mind, and an attitude that says they are going to stop living just to please themselves and start living to please God.

The Lord Jesus, God's Son

If they believe in the Lord Jesus Christ they will be saved. Scriptural references: Acts 21, and many, many more.

I try not to take anything for granted, and knowing that some have been taught nothing in their homes about the Lord Jesus, and taught wrong concepts and ideas in their schools, I try to explain in a few simple sentences who Jesus is.

I begin by saying that the world was in a mess. Satan (the devil) who is against God and all that is good, but nowhere near as powerful as God, fooled many into following him and his evil ways, just as he does today. But Father God so loved people that even though they were not being obedient to him he sent his only Son Jesus down to earth to show them how good life could be if they lived in a way that pleased him.

I go into quite a bit of detail about how the so-called religious people of the time couldn't cope with the Lord Jesus because he showed them up for the wicked people they really were. I also explain that they rigged up a false trial, that they were happy to watch Jesus being beaten up, and that even as he suffered excruciating pain as he was nailed to a wooden cross they still felt no guilt or shame.

Then I ask the children, 'How would you feel if someone had done that to you when you were innocent? I imagine you would have been shouting things back at them, telling them how unfair they were being. But the Lord Jesus didn't act like that. In fact, he was just the opposite. He loved those who were killing him, and he asked his Father to forgive them because they didn't understand what they were doing.'

Then comes the hardest, yet most important, detail to explain. In the Old Testament animals were a substitute for man, and that is why they were sacrificed to take away the wrong things that man had done. But here on the cross Jesus was the perfect Lamb of God, and as he was being sacrificed to deal with all man's wickedness—past, present and future—even Father God couldn't look at his Son as he carried in his body all mankind's sin.

He didn't deserve to die; we do. Jesus was our substitute and he paid the death penalty for our wrong-doing.

As Satan saw Jesus dying on the cross he was thrilled because he thought that he had destroyed God's Son. But it was then that with his fading breath Jesus shouted out, 'It is finished,' which was not a cry of defeat but a cry of victory. It literally meant, 'My work is completed.' Satan, sin and death need no longer be man's destiny. Jesus through his suffering has unlocked the gates of heaven and offers life without end for those who believe in him.

Being physically dead, Jesus was buried like other men in a tomb, but in those days it was more like a cave and had a big stone rolled over the entrance. But after three days an angel of God rolled away the big stone and when people looked inside there was no dead body to be found because Jesus had come back to life. Over a short while he showed himself to many, even telling them to touch him to prove that he was not a ghost but the real Jesus who had risen from the dead.

This is not a story or a fable; this is the truth. To become a Christian it is important to believe that these things really did happen.

And finally, this means little if we don't allow God to come into our lives and change us.

The Holy Spirit

I continue by saying that Jesus, being in human body like you and me, could only be in one place at one time, so Jesus said that he was going to go back and be with his Father until the time was right for him to come back and wind up man's time on earth for good.

He also said that he wouldn't leave us by ourselves. He would send his Holy Spirit, who, being Spirit, could be everywhere and in everyone at the same time, and that if we invited his Spirit to come and live in our lives, he would not only start changing us so that we could be more like the Lord Jesus, but he would also give us power to live out our lives on earth in a way that pleases God.

After this, it is important to have just a short time where the children can reflect upon what they have heard, pray, and also be encouraged to speak out loud and thank God that he has not only heard their prayers but has also already begun to answer them. Teaching them to speak out loud is again a good starting point; you want them in time to be unafraid to speak out and pray in public.

Although this may sound wordy and too simplistic in parts for the older Christian, I hope you get the point I am making. Just as children and adults have varying degrees of intelligence, so their understanding will vary, but if we present the biblical way of salvation in a way that they can understand, the Holy Spirit will reveal the truth, whatever their mental or physical age.

When a little baby is born into this world it knows nothing and has nearly everything to learn. It is the same when someone is reborn into the family of God and becomes a Christian; they too begin a new life and have nearly everything to learn. The day our miraculous new life begins, we know that a change has taken place—to use a Bible quotation, 'We have passed from death to life'—but it is going to take a little while before we start to understand what exactly has happened. The Christian life is not a one-off experience where we are filled with all knowledge and become instantly perfect; once born we start to develop and grow, and it is as we mature that we start to realise what exactly has happened to us.

It infuriates me when parents see me a few hours later and say that they can see no change in their child, or, worse still, when they confront the child after a slight misdemeanour using such words as, 'Call yourself a Christian?' Internal change is instant, but habits of a lifetime, even of a short lifetime, may take a little while to die.

That is the straightforward bit, which I share with either an individual or a crowd. This may give some clue to the parent who is not sure what to say to their seeking child and is waiting for an itinerant children's evangelist to come along and do the work for them. Expect to see your children become Christians at an early age, and also expect to be the ones who will be introducing them to Jesus and praying with them for their salvation.

This will often happen quite naturally at bath-times or bed-times as you are together. Allow times for questions to flow, especially during or after a bed-time Bible story or while you're enjoying the relaxed atmosphere of lunch after your Sunday meeting. Remember that the actual moment a child decides to become a Christian, whether in the home or in a meeting, is so often a culmination of many little 'chats' that you have been having together. It is important to keep sowing.

Please don't feel that you will be doing us children's workers out of a job if it's you who helps them to become Christians and not us. I often feel that I am doing *you* out of a job. Ephesians 6:4 says, 'Fathers, do not exasperate your children; instead, bring them up in the training and instruction of the Lord.' OK, Mums and Dads, get on with it. Why leave all the blessings to us? You deserve a few of them yourselves.

Moving on from the individual to the larger group, I usually feel it right to give those to whom God is speaking a chance to respond to him in a public way. It's not that I want to embarrass them; it's just that once they have made a stand in front of their friends, declaring that they want to serve God, they do seem a lot stronger for it and, understandably, it is not so hard for them when they start to tell other friends what Jesus means to them. But any sort of appeal involving children has to be thought through.

We evangelists love to quote numbers. It looks very impressive in a newsletter when 'hundreds come to the front'. As well as giving us a sense of security, it also lets others know that we are doing our job well. Personally, numbers have never impressed me, and since working with children I have noticed just how inaccurate headhunters or handcounters can be.

I was in a meeting with about 750 eight- to eleven-year-olds, and after some fun and worship I presented the good news of Jesus to them. While still in quite an emotional atmosphere, I appealed to all those who wanted to give their lives to Jesus for the very first time to stand up and come to the front. Before anyone moved I repeated two more times that it was only for those who had never done this before. The minute I finished speaking, about 350 squeezed their way up to the front, and as I stood on the stage and saw the enormous mass of little heads in front of me, the optimist would have thought that revival had broken out, while the pessimist would have thought that it was pure emotionalism. The truth was it was neither.

As we took the children to one side to pray for them, we discovered that the words I had used in my appeal had changed by the time they had reached these young ears. 'I came forward to keep my friend company,' said one. 'I wanted Ishmael's autograph,' said another. One even commented that we had given him a little booklet the year before, but he feared that when he lost this he may also have lost his salvation, so he thought he had better come forward and get another one.

This is one of the reasons why we get the children to write down on a piece of paper a prayer of thanks to God for what he has done in their lives, for then, and only then, do we start to get a realistic idea of what has actually been happening.

On this evening, out of the 350 initial responders, about 100 children genuinely became Christians for the first time.

This was confirmed by the number of parents I have seen subsequently who have told me of a dramatic change in their children's lives since that evening. That is exciting. As for the rest of the children who responded, I praise God for them too for a couple of reasons.

The first is that we had a chance to pray for them and it's always a great privilege to pray into these little ones' lives. Secondly, it's great that they are not frightened to stand up and walk to the front of a meeting. The church will be much healthier if when these young ones reach adulthood they are still as open to responding. I believe that a lot of adults miss out because they are too embarrassed to respond openly when God speaks to them.

There are, of course, many other ways of finding out those who genuinely would like to be prayed with, or who wish to know more. The most common is the 'hands up, stay where you are' appeal. The only trouble I've personally found with this is that while the Spirit of God is moving in their lives we encourage those who are already Christians to worship the Lord, and of course for many of them nowadays their most natural expression of worship involves raising their hands. It looks great from the front, but unless you are good with your words of knowledge, it is going to be a bit of a job to sort out the sheep from the would-be sheep.

I suppose the most accurate means I have found for finding those who want to become Christians is this, and it involves two things. What you don't do is offer any 'bait' or reward such as a little book, because most children would love a free book, even if once they have seen how boring it is, it ends its life as a paper aeroplane or swept up with the rubbish on the floor. You may still give a book to those who respond afterwards, but you don't advertise the fact that you are giving them away during the appeal. Then, when you have finished sharing the good news with them, just say, 'For those who want to give their lives to Jesus, see me at the end of the meeting.' You only need to say this once. Then do something quite opposite like a real bouncy action song to completely break the emotional atmosphere that you have built up.

I do believe that if the Spirit of God is really moving in a child's life, amid everything that may follow they will remember to come and see you after the meeting. I have proved this to be true. This is ideal for the smaller children's meeting which is held at regular intervals, where you have already built up a good relationship with your children, but weekly appeals become repetitious.

Finally, a few hints for when you are leading an evangelistic meeting:

(1) For those who have responded, it is good to get them to pray a prayer after you. It is important that you keep it short and speak slowly. I remember the first time that I did this I spoke so quickly and with such long sentences that the children could not keep up with me, nor could they remember the sentence that I told them to repeat. Worse than that, neither could I.

(2) Never under any circumstances take children out to another room to pray for them. Non-Christian parents are very suspicious of Christians nowadays (and understandably so) because of all the adverse press that we have been given. Be open, let people see what you are doing, and if they are nearby, invite them to join you as you pray.

(3) When a child from a non-Christian background gives his life to Christ, someone needs to go and talk it through with the parents. Don't just leave it to the child to explain, as he may accidentally say all sorts of things that will horrify the parents. Send round your best evangelist; a great opportunity!

(4) Don't forget to teach the children that what they have

received they need to share. Also teach them how to share it. They will be better than any schools workers as they get alongside friends of their own age. Oversee them, but don't feel that you have to be for ever walking behind them to see if they are saying the right words and doing it the way you would do it. They probably won't be. They are children and it is quite normal for them to say things in a childish way. If we have trained them well they will portray God's heart, if not our words, and there will not only be a lot more labourers going into the harvest field, but there will also be a lot more crops coming into the barn. Yes, God has put no age limit on his workers and neither should we.

14
Creating a Home

Anona Coates

Anona is married to Gerald and they have three sons, Paul and Simon living away from home with friends, and Jonathan, still at home. Anona feels her main role has been to provide a secure home and family for Gerald upon his return from national and international events. She has also been highly successful at relating to unbelievers and drawing them into the Christian community. This chapter is reproduced by permission from her book Creativity *(© Christian Woman 1985, published by Triangle/SPCK).*

Home at its best should be the one place where we can relax and be ourselves; where we are able to withdraw from the pressures of the outside world and draw strength from the people closest to us. And for any Christian home to operate properly there must be order. God is the ultimate head of the house. Then he has ordained the husband to be the earthly and spiritual head, loving and caring for the wife and children. The wife is to be subject to her husband and the Lord, and the children to respect parental authority, being brought up in God's love (Eph 5:22–23; 6:1–4). This is God's purpose for us and, with the help of the Holy Spirit living through us, it is not as impossible as it sounds! The rewards of living properly are terrific, promoting peaceful co-existence and the security that we all need, allowing us to be ourselves in God. And you are not to feel left out if you are unmarried, divorced or widowed. God's plan for you is just as important—elders or leaders in the church are to provide the care and covering you need (1 Pet 5:5; 1 Tim 5:1–16).

A home is more than a building and furniture. Unless we get the foundations of our home life right, no amount of decoration and beautiful furniture will cover the cracks that will appear. One of the unhappiest couples I know, proudly show off their tasteful and comfortable house, but the terrible sadness between them gives the place an empty, hollow atmosphere.

No woman need feel she has nothing to contribute to home-making. If our warmth, love and care are genuine, they will come out in all we do. You may feel you are not creative: 'I can't paint a watercolour, I've never even written a poem, I'm just not artistic.' Some people do have a natural ability to put colours together, arrange furniture and ornaments without really trying—we call that style. Most of us lesser mortals have to work harder, but we can still enjoy creating our own individual atmosphere and style.

We are all creative beings, and we have been created in God's image (Gen 1:27). He is of course the Creator *par excellence*. He has put within us the ability to create, whatever we are doing. In fact we are always creating whether we like it or not. We create either a good impression or a bad impression with people. We create a warm welcoming environment or a cold unfriendly one. Let's not be satisfied with mediocre lives and homes; let's use the gifts God has given us to our best ability, stretching our capacity to be creative. In the parable of the talents we read that the Lord is pleased when we multiply the gifts he has given us.

Tied down

There is no need for the modern woman to be tied to the kitchen sink. Many combine a satisfying job with a good home life. It can be very stimulating to have an outside interest. But do remember, someone else can do your outside job, but no one else can take your place in the important role of wife and mother.

A marvellous example of the kind of woman we should try to emulate can be found in Proverbs 31:10–31. Translated into modern terms I see her as a model of the kind of woman I would like to be. Her husband can rely on her; he has an important job and is a leader in the community, so he needs to know she will not be a drag on him but will support him. When he returns home exhausted she has almost everything under control. The house is straight, the children in order, and she looks good—even if it isn't her best! She is the kind of person you ask for advice, knowing she'll answer wisely—she is obviously a good mother, taking a real interest in her children. She is a very good business-woman and disciplined in her work, certainly not lazy—laziness isn't a virtue. She also cares for the poor and needy, supports various charities and gives out whatever she has, even if it hurts sometimes.

If this gives you a picture of a 'do-gooder', well why not? I would rather be a 'do-gooder' than a 'do-badder' or a 'do-nothing-at-all'. 'It's all right for her,' I hear some say. 'I have to go out to work. How can I keep the house tidy with three children under four years?' Or, 'My husband never helps in the house, I have to cope with everything.'

I can appreciate how you feel. Over the years I have brought up three sons, had countless friends living with us, my husband has worked from home and, worst of all, we have had a very hairy dog as part of the family. It is not easy always to have the house spotless, clothes washed and ironed, plenty of food prepared, and to look immaculate at the same time. The secret is to decide what we want our home life to be like: are we going to muddle on, letting the situation dictate to us? Or are we going to decide to change the situation and be in control?

If the latter is the case, the first step is to get organised. Sit down with a notebook and list your priorities. If you are taking on too much, something must go. You don't want your whole life to be taken up with housework and home-making. Put the housework in its place so it can serve you and not rule you. Work out a routine. This will be different for everyone. Let it fit your lifestyle, leaving you plenty of time to spend with God, your husband and

children if you have them, friends and family, and to pursue the
other interests you have. Do all the essential jobs regularly, then
if something unplanned comes up you can always catch up on the
housework later.

Opening your home

Now we have started to get our family life in order and our
housework under control, we can happily open our home to
others. Hospitality is not an optional extra for a Christian, but a
command from the Lord (Rom 12:13). When Gerald and I
married, the minister officiating at our wedding spoke of Lazarus,
Martha and Mary opening their home to the Lord and his
disciples. He encouraged us to do the same. It certainly was a
prophetic word. From the minute we moved into our own house,
the Lord sent people to share it with us. This has been a great
blessing to us as well as to others. It has been marvellous for the
children to grow up with other people, to learn from them and to
enjoy their company.

You may not have the room to have people living with you
permanently, but hospitality can be shown in many ways. Having
folk to stay with you for a week or two, or just for an evening
meal or maybe a weekend, has many rewards. Do not wait until
you can afford to be hospitable; many widows and single people
who have very little, excel in hospitality. You don't have to be
extravagant; simply share what you have and God will bless you
for it. It is important that your attitude is right to your guests. Tell
them what you have to offer gladly.

Welcoming guests

Depending on the time of day and the reason for the visit, your
response to visitors will vary. If a neighbour or friend is just
popping in to see you, to borrow something or to ask advice, an
offer of tea, coffee or a cold drink and maybe biscuits or cake is
quite sufficient. They have not come to eat or drink, but to see
you. On the other hand, if you have invited friends for an informal

meal, lunch, tea or supper, you will want to give more thought and preparation. I have found that cold meats and cheeses, salads, jacket potatoes, quiches and a selection of fruit are some of the many dishes which do not entail too much preparation. If you enjoy baking, home-made cakes and biscuits are a real treat. Keep your eyes open, when shopping, for the more unusual foods that are available in small delicatessens or large supermarkets. My local supermarket has an amazing selection of seafoods, exotic fruits and vegetables and many different kinds of bread. Indian and Chinese food is becoming more popular and all the ingredients are now available in the shops. Don't be afraid to experiment— but not on your guests! It's not a good idea to try out a complicated new dish when you are expecting eight people you don't know well. Do check on people's tastes and special diets too.

Put thought and care into presenting the food. Even the most humble meal can look very appetising if carefully laid out and served well. People will realise you care without saying a word. Your china is very important here. Even if you don't have a complete dinner and tea service, check your china and glass for cracks and keep back any that are not in good condition. As well as being unhygienic, it is an insult to your family and friends to serve up food on chipped and stained china.

You do not need to spend a fortune on your crockery. Sale time is an ideal time to buy china—very expensive sets are often drastically reduced. Plain white china is even cheaper and can looked very effective mixed with patterned pieces or some of a contrasting colour. Do not buy anything too fashionable as it will date very quickly; and choose colours which blend with the rooms you will be using it in. Plastic, although fine for storage, is not ideal for use at the table, except for children. Likewise, paper plates are so difficult to eat from; I prefer to keep them for picnics.

If you have guests for a formal meal, here is your chance to be even more creative than usual. There are a great many interesting cookery books available. If you cannot afford to buy them yourself, borrow them from your local library, and keep special favourite recipes cut from magazines. Don't be afraid to ask friends for their recipes if you really enjoyed a particular meal.

Planning

Plan well ahead if you don't want to be exhausted and dishevelled by the time your guests arrive. You won't enjoy the evening and they will feel like an intrusion and bother to you. If your days are busy with work or caring for children, it is a great help if you can shop for and prepare some of the food a few days before. A freezer is very helpful here; perhaps you could borrow space in a neighbour's or friend's freezer if you do not have your own.

First, sit down with pen, paper and any cookery books you have and think about the guests. Consider their tastes and appetites if you know them; if not, stick to reasonably ordinary dishes, but not boring ones. Are you good at cooking one particular kind of dish? One friend of mine enjoys and excels in making Indian curries. It is a real treat for all her guests to eat a meal that they themselves would perhaps never cook at home.

Keep the 'starter', if you are having one, light; it can be unusual but not too filling. You will want your guests to enjoy the main course. A variety of seasonable vegetables served well will complement the meat or fish. If you are vegetarian you will have your own favourite recipes. Most of us are aware of the amount of sugar and fat we consume, so consider this when planning the meal, the sweet in particular. Go easy on the cream and sugar. Unless you and your guests are teetotal, offer wine, fruit juice and mineral water with the meal.

The kind of food and drink you serve often has to be guided by the amount of money you can spend. Mince, served with love and care, can taste much better than steak. It really is not that important how much the meal costs. If your guests leave the house refreshed in mind, body and spirit, you've done a great job. Again, it is the little touches you as the hostess make that contribute to the evening. It certainly helps if the house is clean and tidy. (Don't forget the toilet and bathroom here, and put out fresh towels for your guests.) Low lighting can be very restful in the evening, especially if you use candles on the table. But remember to put them out when you leave the room; we have nearly burned the house down twice by forgetting them!

Check that your guests are warm enough—it's very hard to enjoy a meal if you are shivering. If your dining chairs are not particularly comfortable, adjourn to something softer as soon as you have finished eating and serve coffee in a more relaxing situation. Music also serves to relax us and is great to have on in the background. Think of any other ways you can bless and encourage your visitors—perhaps a small gift, posy of flowers or single rose on a plate with their place setting at the table.

Should guests help with the washing up? It really is up to you. Judge each situation differently. I usually prefer to clear most of the pots and pans before the meal and wash up the rest afterwards. Sometimes, though, you can sense folk would really like to help, to feel more involved; or perhaps they find it easier to talk and share while doing something. Just be sensitive to the situation— either way, serve your guests.

If you personally are having a marvellous time, don't prolong the evening unreasonably if your guests have to be up early next morning. They will not thank you for keeping them too late. My husband and I have often visited friends for a meal, really enjoyed the evening, and then just as we were about to leave, our host or hostess has suddenly announced, 'We really want to talk to you. We have this problem.' This is a mistake. If you want to talk seriously, start much earlier in the evening, before your guests are tired and ready for their beds.

Sometimes we get into a rut, when even though we want to be hospitable, having people to meals or coffee is all we can think of doing. Let's be more creative in our hospitality. Taking part in some activity together is very rewarding. If you and a friend or neighbour both enjoy the same hobby, get together to do it, perhaps one week at one house and the next week, the other. Many a small business has started like this. A friend and myself started a little business selling herbs and spices, pot-pourri, pillows and lavender bags. As well as attending markets and church groups we also visit homes where in an informal way we give a talk on the uses of herbs and spices and then offer the items for sale. As we have packaged and made everything ourselves we can keep the prices really low and no one is embarrassed into spending too much money. This gives us a marvellous opportunity to meet new friends and we often have a chance to share our faith with them.

Other people I know like to get together to pray and study the Bible and perhaps include other friends who are not Christians. If you do this, do not feel you must keep meeting together for years when the need and circumstances change; be free enough to change with them.

Another good way to express your friendship to people is to invite them to your home for a 'party'—but not the normal type. You could invite someone to give a short talk or demonstration on a subject that would interest your visitors. Perhaps you could have things for sale—we all know the companies whose representatives will visit your home. The only reservation I have is that some of the items are very expensive and we do not want to put pressure on people to spend money they do not have on things they do not need.

If you move to a new area, a party would be a very useful way of getting to know your new neighbours. Perhaps you know someone who makes soft toys, pictures and cards with dried flowers, or jewellery—include them in. Arrange an 'open-day' or 'open-evening', invite twice as many people as you would like to come, prepare refreshments, and don't forget to introduce people to one another.

Long-term hospitality

Most of us at times like to offer hospitality over a longer period, with guests staying with us overnight or for a week or two. Most homes do not allow enough rooms for one to be used exclusively for guests. It is more a matter of *how* you accommodate your guests than where. A sofa bed in a study or living room can be very useful, but please do not sit up until midnight watching your favourite television programme when your guest is longing for rest and privacy. A single person would probably be very happy on a temporary bed for a night or two, but if it is for any longer, or you have a married couple staying, I recommend you give them your bedroom. I am not talking about long-term visitors in an extended family situation; something more permanent must be arranged then.

We must consider the reason our guests are with us. Perhaps it is for a rest and holiday, or perhaps they are ministering to the church in some way. They will need privacy, comfort, peace and quiet when they want it. In her excellent book, *The Pleasure of Your Company*, Dale Garratt shares how important hospitality is to the Christian and gives many examples of showing honour to our guests. My husband has stayed with the Garratt family in New Zealand and has sampled first hand their wonderful kindness and generosity.

Before your guests arrive, decide where they will be sleeping and write a list of items you will need and the jobs to be done to make their stay pleasant and comfortable. Here is an example of my list to give you some ideas:

1. Make up the bed with fresh linen.
2. Dust and vacuum the room.
3. Air the room and heat if necessary.
4. Clear space in drawers and wardrobe for clothing. Supply hangers.
5. Provide bath and hand towels for each person.
6. Place in the room a plant or fresh flowers.
7. Place in the room a bowl of fruit and chocolates.
8. Provide a jug of water or bottle of mineral water and glasses.
9. Provide tissues.
10. Books or magazines.
11. Notepaper, envelopes, stamps and pens.
12. A little note or card welcoming your guests.

I am sure you can think of many other ideas—perhaps something to nibble, or a basket containing small bottles of bubble bath, perfume or aftershave, and an emergency sewing kit.

Some visitors may appreciate a hot-water bottle or an extra blanket, particularly if they are older folk. An electric kettle and cups and saucers to make tea or coffee are again an ideal facility for older people, or for visitors who may not feel free enough to pop into the kitchen whenever they feel like a cup of tea.

After your guests have arrived, had a refreshing drink and recovered from the journey, show them to their room and around the rest of the house, particularly the bathroom and toilet. Point out anything they need to know—most houses have their own little quirks. It is better to know beforehand that the toilet blocks easily or the bathroom door jams unless you push it from the bottom! Before they settle down for the night, check that they have everything they need and discuss plans for breakfast.

After experiencing many homes all over the world, I have learned that one of the most difficult times can be at breakfast. Either you get up and wander around the house looking for someone, wondering whether you ought to help yourself, or you are presented with a three-course cooked breakfast which you never normally eat but feel you must tackle as your hostess has gone to so much trouble. Good hospitality is not forcing as much food as possible into your visitors by emotional blackmail. Find out what their appetite is like and which foods they particularly enjoy.

Most people, when staying with a family, like to join in and feel part of it, perhaps enjoying your children if they have none of their own. But be aware; other people's children can be very exhausting sometimes, and although you want the children to show hospitality in their own way, do not let them pester the guests. Try to teach them to be welcoming and friendly, but not pushy.

A while ago I thought I had better check that our three sons did not mind us having so many visitors in their home. They looked at me in astonishment when I asked them—it certainly did not bother them. In fact, they were often quite upset when people who had stayed for a week left, just as they have become close friends. I really hope and pray that our children will be able to learn from us and that, now they are getting older and starting out in their own homes, showing hospitality will come more naturally to them than it has to us. Many of us have been brought up in homes where, however good they are in other ways, welcoming friends and strangers has not been the normal way of life. So we have had to learn the hard way, to open up ourselves as well as our homes. This is not always achieved without pain; the more we open ourselves to others, the more vulnerable we are, the more likely we are to be hurt and sometimes misused.

We must also be prepared for the Lord and his 'willing helpers', our friends, to make adjustments in our lives when necessary. Our homes and our families are very precious to us and any criticism of them we take very personally. But let's be open to God to take us on one step at a time and aim at creating in our homes and families the kind of situation where we can show the kingdom of God.

Back to the house

Even if the place where you are living is not ideal, please do not wait for the perfect house, the cottage you have always dreamed of, or the brand new town house you long for. Make your home where you are now. For a start you are learning, and perhaps making mistakes when it does not matter too much. It is important that you have, however humble, a room or bedsit that reflects you and your personality. Do not allow yourself to sit in a dull, boring room dreaming of what you would like one day; this only breeds dissatisfaction and depression.

The way in which we arrange and decorate our home is an expression of our personality and should reflect the artistry and order which is in God's creation.

If we take time to look at God's natural creation, we can see how perfectly the colours, shades and textures blend together. Just as we are relaxing and being inwardly refreshed by the harmony of colour, our breath is taken away by a brilliant splash of colour. It may be a sunset, blossom on the trees, or a mass of colourful flowers. Scaled down, this principle is a useful starting point when planning a colour scheme for a room.

There are three primary colours: red, yellow and blue. All other colours are derived from them. If red and yellow are mixed we have orange; blue and red gives purple, and blue and yellow produces green. Add black to these colours and they darken; white, of course, will lighten them. If you blend a little of one colour with another, you will produce a shade which will blend with either of them. If this all sounds rather complicated, try to obtain a colour wheel from a decorator's shop or a magazine; they are very useful. As well as showing you the colours which harmonise, you can clearly see the contrasting colour which, if added in a small amount, say in a cushion or pictures, can make an ordinary room much more interesting. Remember the sunset or blossom and the impact it had.

Your choice of colour will make a difference to the apparent size of the room. Warm darker colours will 'advance' towards you, making the room feel smaller. Light, cool colours 'retreat' and the room seems larger.

Even if you cannot decorate a rented home, there are many other ways of enhancing it. Don't do anything too expensive or permanent—you may have to leave it behind.

If you collect things as a hobby, group them together to make an interesting display. Use a shape—a triangle, oblong, square or circle—as a guide when displaying objects. For example, a tall vase with smaller ornaments either side is easy on the eye. If you cannot hang pictures on the walls, prop them up on the mantelpiece or on a shelf, even on the floor next to a large plant or vase of dried flowers. A screen, homemade or bought, can be used to hide a kitchen area in a small flat or to cut off part of a room. If the carpet is dirty or worn, cover it with cheap, bright rugs. Lots of cushions and plants will make the room warmer.

Storage is often a problem in a small home, so only keep what you need. My own rule is: if I haven't used it or worn it in the last two years I probably never will, and can do without it. We often surround ourselves with so much clutter that perhaps someone else could use.

Remember to keep your room or rooms tidy. I know it's a hard discipline, especially if you live on your own, but well worth it. Think how much freer you will be to invite a friend back for coffee if you know the bed is made, the dishes are washed, and there are no dirty undies lying around the room. Make your home a place to be proud of.

Room by room

Let's go through an average house and look at ideas for each room. I am not assuming everyone has a house. Just pick out the parts that apply to your home and adapt them for your own use.

The hall is an often-neglected but very important area. It is the first part of your home guests see—it needs to be welcoming. In most parts of Britain we need a much warmer welcome, and I don't just mean a radiator, although the hall is often forgotten when central heating is put in a house. Warm colours you could use here include red, orange, yellow, peach and plum.

The walls and flooring in a hall will take quite a battering, so washable paint or wallpaper is recommended. The flooring needs to be practical—tiles of various kinds: quarry, flagstones or slate. If you are fortunate enough to live in a Victorian or Edwardian house with an old-fashioned tiled floor, do not cover it up but make it the main feature. I was thrilled with the beautiful stone floor we had in a previous house. It lasted for eighty years and still looked special.

Bare boards, scraped, sanded and sealed look good, but if you add rugs, be sure they cannot slip and cause accidents. Fasten them with Velcro or the special sticky tape you can obtain from carpet shops. Many halls are long and thin, so a mirror and some hooks for coats are really all you can fit in. A group of pictures or some unusual plates can add interest and take up no more than wall space. If the area is wider, you can add furniture, maybe a chair, a table or chest of drawers with a plant or a vase of dried or fresh flowers.

You will notice I am always mentioning plants and flowers. They make such a difference to a room. Half-dead plants look terrible, though, so if they cannot be revived, dispose of them. Cut flowers can be expensive, but a small arrangement of wild flowers can be just as effective. If you are unsure about arranging flowers, borrow a book from your local library to help you. Learn a new art form. Dried flowers can be bought at markets and bazaars very cheaply. Once, at a 'sports day' stall, for £2.00 I bought a bunch of 'Honesty' so large it would not fit into the car. You can dry your own flowers from the garden and give some away as gifts.

Containers make all the difference to plants and flowers. Gradually gather a collection which fit in your home and can be used together. Green plants of varying sizes and textures look especially good grouped together. Plants are the most useful accessory you can have, adding colour, height, variety and drama to a room.

The main living room is often the hardest room to design. You really need to think carefully before you start on this room. Make a list of everything, your general ideas, colour scheme and so on, and draw a diagram. You need to ask yourself several questions. How much can you afford to spend on the room? Do you want to start from scratch or by choosing, say, a new carpet or new seating, can you revitalise the whole room? If everything is in good condition but you are a little bored with the room, just by adding different coloured cushion covers, a new lamp shade and rearranging your accessories, you can change the whole mood of things.

Think carefully about your use of the room. Will you be eating in it, needing a table and dining chairs? Will you be watching television and listening to music? The furniture must be suitably positioned. If it will be used purely for entertaining and talking, the chairs are best placed at right angles with perhaps a couple of low tables. You may need plenty of floor space for children to spread out on with their toys. Will you need storage space? Can you use either the normal shop-bought storage units or put up glass shelves for a lighter look? An unusual idea, if you have the space, is to buy a large Victorian wardrobe and adapt it to living room use.

If you are starting from scratch and can plan a colour scheme, pick your main colour and gradually build up a collection of material and carpet samples and paint or wallpaper cards in shades of that colour. Look at them regularly. If you begin to tire of them, it will be a good idea to change your scheme at this stage, before you have made an expensive mistake. And on the subject of expense, it is wise to have a budget and stick to it. Although we often think it would be nice to have an endless supply of money, the choice of goods would be so vast it would be far harder to decide what we really want.

Once you have decided on the amount you can spend, start to look around the shops, particularly during sale time—huge savings can be made and you may be able to buy better quality goods than you had planned.

Do make sure that jobs like rewiring and plastering are done by an expert before you start to decorate. Then, as the room begins to take shape, you can start to add the extras which make it your home and not a carbon copy of a shop window. You will already have possessions which will fit in the room—books, plates, ornaments and so on. Many people enjoy collecting objects which interest them. The way we arrange our collections is important. Do not let your accessories become static. Move them around regularly; experiment with them.

Always be on the lookout for new ideas to enhance your home. Be aware of other people's décor, and don't be shy about asking for advice—most people would be thrilled if you admircd their taste. Make use of magazines and books. You may not be able to afford the actual items pictured, but take a room set they have used and scale it down to fit your home and budget. Department store windows, hotels and stately homes can also be a source of fresh ideas.

Time for a rest!

Now the main bedroom. If you do not share this room, here is your chance really to indulge yourself. On the other hand, if you are married, temper your desire to fill the room with pink lace cushions—it might be a little too much for your husband.

If you are faced with a bare room and are not sure where to

start, you could build the room around a favourite item, a beautiful lace bedspread, a mirror or a particular piece of furniture. Or you could pick on an era or style—Victoriana, art deco, country style—something that is you and that suits the house. It would look rather peculiar to have a pretty Laura Ashley style bedroom in an ultra-modern split-level dwelling, or art deco in a fifteenth-century farmhouse.

The shops are filled with beautifully matched bedroom sets, from wallpaper through bed linen to tissue box holders. Although these are a marvellous help in co-ordinating the room, be very careful not to overfill the room with one design—complement patterned items with plain colours and different textures.

The bedroom is the one room where you can lay a pale carpet and not 'fear to tread'.

Keep lighting soft and restful, with more direct light where it is needed for reading or applying make-up. When buying new furniture for a bedroom, comfort should be your main consideration. If necessary, spend most of your budget on the bed. It really is important; you will spend a lot of your life lying on it. Many people use duvets instead of blankets now. If you are thinking of changing, ask a friend if you can borrow theirs, perhaps while they are on holiday, and try it out for a week or two before investing a lot of money.

If the room is large enough, add a table or desk and chairs which can be used for studying or sewing. For extra storage use small chests of drawers instead of bedside cabinets, and place shelves or cupboards in alcoves. If you install fitted wardrobes and cupboards, take them up to the ceiling—utilise all the space you can.

Children's rooms will ideally grow with the child. When planning the room, keep in mind the modifications you will need to make over the years. Children love bright colours and enjoy having their toys and possessions on display. Once you have satisfied yourself the room is safe and practical, do let the child have a say in the décor and planning. As children grow older their taste will change and develop. Do let them experiment, even if it's not your idea of how a bedroom should be. We all appreciate a place of our own and enjoy the fun of putting it together.

Bathrooms and toilets can often be the forgotten rooms when we think of interior design, but with a little imagination, we can transform them into interesting rooms. If you are investing in new bathroom facilities, think carefully about what you need before you buy. Measure the space available and ask your plumber's advice; you might be able to place the bath in the middle of the room, or add a bidet or shower.

Remember, a white bathroom suite is much cheaper than coloured and will look terrific with bright primary colours added on the walls or in the towels and accessories. With the more subtly-coloured suites, toning pastel colours will look particularly good. You can use your imagination when planning the style of the bathroom, but if it leads off or is next to a bedroom, try to tie the two rooms together in colouring and design.

What's cooking?

Everyone's idea of the perfect kitchen is different. If you are out at work all day and do not particularly enjoy cooking, a plain, functional, well-planned kitchen will satisfy your needs. On the other hand, if you love to spend all your spare time in the kitchen and use it as the hub of the home where family and friends congregate, you will need a much more comfortable, homely room. For you it would be worth knocking down a wall and combining the dining area and perhaps even adding easy chairs to make it into the main living room.

Whatever your needs, the same principle of planning applies here. Think long and hard before you shop, especially before you buy costly equipment. Make lists of the things you need, think of the appliances you would like to add in the future, leave space for them on your plan of the room. Shop around different firms for the best buys, especially during sales.

We never seem to have enough work surfaces, storage space or electric sockets, so if you are planning a fitted kitchen, take these into consideration. You may have the chance to purchase new fitted units and appliances—that's marvellous—but be careful not to choose anything too gimmicky; you will be living with it for many years.

Most of us inherit a kitchen which we cannot afford to dispose of, but we would like to change it and add character. Here are a few tips:

1. Remove old units and replace with pine cupboards and dressers. If there is room, add a pine table and chairs.
2. Fit new doors and work surfaces.
3. Change handles on doors to brass or colourful plastic ones.
4. Replace old curtains with blinds or cafe curtains.
5. Lay new flooring, preferably tiles or vinyl.
6. Add colourful accessories: storage jars, kitchen-roll holders, spice racks, tea towels, washing-up bowl, etc.
7. Paint the walls or add some interesting tiles.
8. Don't forget the less functional accessories which will add interest: bunches of herbs or dried flowers, plants, baskets, pictures, etc.

I am sure you will think of many more ideas—not just for the kitchen, but for your home in general. Don't just think though—put them into action.

My final thought

Never let the interior design of your home be your main pre-occupation. It is just part of our lives in which we can be creative and enjoy the abundant life God has given us. Homes are for people—let's help them feel at home.

15

Maintaining Our Cutting Edge

Gerald Coates

Gerald Coates is Director of the Pioneer Trust and leader of the Pioneer team. Their main role is to care for churches in a partnership relationship, plant churches, and train leaders and evangelists through their TIE (Training In Evangelism) Teams. He is known as a speaker both nationally and internationally, and has written six books, including his autobiography An Intelligent Fire *and* Kingdom Now! *a more detailed manifesto than is contained in his two chapters in this book.*

A blurred message or set of policies will only ever attract the attention of the uncommitted. Sharpness is of necessity. I recently addressed a fraternal of clergy. A few were evangelical who were preaching the gospel leading to conversion. The majority were liberals, modernists and universalists. They were quite offended when I gently told them that their good news was bad news; that it was confused news and not viable news. Then an amazing twist took place. My fellow evangelicals present at the meeting began to tell me how nice and kind these liberals were; how charming they had found one another. Subjective warmth and respect soon became confused with the objective message of the gospel. The fact the majority didn't believe much that was in the Bible didn't really matter as they were such 'nice blokes'. They then explained they were about to embark on a mission. 'What on earth will your message be?' I asked. Their message was a very acceptable 'God loves us all'—which is true, but it is not the full gospel. Theologically they were blurred. But they could not work out why all their churches were shrinking numerically!

In our first chapter I mentioned that a prominent Anglican leader from Singapore spoke in our Cobham Christian Fellowship. In 1975–76 3% of his nation were confessing Christians. By 1992 over 15% were Christian. Why? The church, its leaders and members had a clear conversion, a clear message that demanded a clear response. Clarity was the essence.

If we are going to reach this entire nation by the year 2000 we shall need to maintain a clear message. It is not the message of the fellowship—'Come and join us, we're the best, and you'll be blessed.' It is not the message of tradition—'Come and join us and do it our way, the longest-standing way, and you'll be blessed.' It is not the message of the charismatic movement—'Get baptised in the Holy Spirit, speak in tongues and you'll be blessed.' It is the message of the gospel. The gospel that says, 'Repent, believe, be baptised, and be filled with the Spirit.' The gospel that also breaks down racism, sexism and nationalism. The gospel which enables us to love people as we love ourselves, to do for others as we would have them do for us. But if we are going to have a sharp edge in our message, every member of the body of Christ must be familiar with the gospel facts and the gospel story.

Humanity is in rebellion against God, not merely sick (though it is that). Humanity is living independently of God, its Creator and Saviour. Jesus was kind enough to leave the splendours of heaven and be birthed in the space-time world, growing up through babyhood, boyhood and teenage years into a man. He lived perfectly, pleasing his Father at all times. Anointed by the Spirit he talked about his Father in heaven with regard to his nature (what God is like) and his purpose on the earth, his kingdom (what God is doing). He walked through the promised land forgiving sinners, healing the sick, bringing good news to the poor, the marginalised and the oppressed. And then he offered himself as a sacrifice, a substitute for every repentant wrong-doer who would ever come to him asking for forgiveness.

Today, whoever believes that wonderful story about the birth, life, death, resurrection and ascension of Christ into heaven, and is willing to confess Jesus as Lord, can be saved. Saved from hell, continual sin, a life without God. Saved from themselves and into a loving relationship with Jesus Christ. We are not animals (purely earthly) nor angels (purely heavenly) but human beings, saved by God's mercy and grace, straddling the heavenly and the earthly. Our role is to imprint the beauty, power, glory and truth of heaven into the earth by our words and actions.

To maintain a clear edge we must maintain a clear message. It must never be obliterated or put on the back boiler by 'current truth', religious 'buzz' words or church life, however precious and meaningful.

Character and integrity

It was Charles Spurgeon who recommended that Christians in places of responsibility of leadership who dishonoured the call should step out of responsibility, sit at the back of the meetings 'and stay there until their repentance is as notorious as their sins'. We are talking here about maintaining a cutting edge through character development as well as personal and corporate integrity.

We can hardly be expected to maintain a cutting edge while counselling people with lust problems if we are fantasising about other women every time we are intimate with our partners. We can hardly be expected to succeed in godly leadership and talk about financial integrity when we are deliberately sending the Inland Revenue false data with regard to our personal income or church affairs. Those of us in full-time leadership cannot indulge ourselves in the luxury of pocketing gifts as 'personal' when they are clearly 'in payment for work done'.

Christians are often better at cover-up than others! This is because we are often forced to talk further than we are able to walk. I have spoken in many of England's Bible colleges. I've always been told about gifted speakers, up-and-coming theologians and evangelistically gifted students. I often feel like asking, 'Can anyone speak of the personal integrity of these students?' Giftedness builds up, but a lack of character quickly destroys.

There are of course tell-tale signs. First, does a person distance himself from close peers? While the first step towards a moral dilemma consists of distancing ourselves from God, it is often difficult to detect. But the next step is distancing ourselves from our peers. We become lonely. Cover-up is the name of the game. We're ministering and praying for one thing, but living for something else. We will eventually reap what we sow—it's an unalterable law. The usual reaction when someone confronts us with our lack of integrity is to deny the specific situation, excuse ourselves and invariably express hurt or anger with the accuser. (Hurt always attracts sympathy, whereas anger separates.)

I've had kind, compassionate, hard-working Christian leaders come to see me over many years. 'I can't live with this cover-up any longer,' they say as they unburden themselves. One leader took a girl from his church to bed. For years no one had found out. To him it was worse than being found out. It nearly drove him crazy. One youth leader occasionally visited toilets and submitted to being abused by his pick-up for half an hour. His brief experience of pleasure created powerlessness, uselessness, inadequacy and shame when it came to serving God. One pastor knew that if his personal and financial affairs were looked into by the tax office, he would not only be in the newspapers but maybe in prison. The sins we employ in covering up issues are invariably worse than the original sin we committed. We employ lies, deception, pretence, and create a long-term world of religious fantasy.

Sadly, many people who have to be disciplined become isolated or choose a handful of undiscerning friends they can dominate. But each of us is morally responsible for our actions. We are the sum total of all the decisions we have ever made. As I look at myself in the mirror that is a sobering thought! We can't take refuge in our anointing, denomination (or non-denomination), team or happy family. There is no escape. God sees things as they are and one day we shall have to give an account. Quite what that means I am not sure. It's clearly not the same as judgement that leads to hell. But whatever it is, it isn't good. I'd rather be judged now and face a short, sharp shock than live with a dull, heavy inward ache that comes through cover-up.

We must always model the truth, set a caring moral example and close the credibility gap. Even then there is no guarantee we shall bless and influence all we hope for.

As Chuck Swindoll has said, 'There has been only one perfect father and he has a lot of wayward kids.' Ultimately we're all responsible for ourselves. We can't be fully responsible even for our kids as they grow up. Conversely, despite our own background we cannot blame our parents. We may have had a bad start in life. Jesus gives us fresh opportunities and beginnings every day we wake. For too long we have settled for this less-than-holy priesthood. But if we are going to maintain a cutting edge we must aim for excellence in character, asking God's grace and mercy to cover us for past wrongs, confessing them wherever necessary and making restitution where we can.

Black and white?

It is of course possible to be strictly moral while being terribly unethical. We should always ask, 'Is this opportunity a step towards sin even though in and of itself it may not be sin?' Leaders like myself are occasionally given gifts from those we've helped. Some are longstanding friends. Others give us something by way of a small gift of personal financial blessing towards our family as a result of being away from home so much. We rarely see most of these folk again. But what if the gifts are frequent? What happens when we become grateful, begin to 'connect' emotionally? We then become obligated. The person then often transfers their affections and needs to us. Our continual acceptance of those gifts nurtures dependence on us and the time we are giving them. We are hooked. We then feel we have to respond, fulfil our obligations

towards them and, in the light of their gifts, give them the time
they want. The character of the Holy Spirit goes out of the
window.

Is it immoral to receive gifts? Obviously not. Scripture says that
it is better to give than to receive. If nobody will receive, there'll
be nobody to give to! But while receiving gifts may not be
immoral, it may at times be unethical. Hardline evangelists tend
to think of integrity and immorality in terms of what is sin and
what is not sin. This is not always helpful. It is certainly inadequate.
We do of course take our morality from Scripture. In the light of
Scripture we also take it from common-sense experience. I don't
need Scripture to tell me that to do 90mph through our High
Street is wrong.

The more we want to define what sin is and what it is not, the
greater the temptation to abandon ethics. If it is wrong for me to
drink wine, I make it wrong for everyone else. Conversely, if it is
not sin, other people, whatever their convictions or preferences,
will have to put up with my liberty. Both are unethical. Integrity
has to do with ethics and sensitivity to others, as well as black-
and-white morality.

Dangerous territory

I suppose morality can be looked upon much like the edge of a
cliff. On one side is the 'not sin' territory. But one wrong step and
it's 'into sin' and disaster. A personal or corporate code of ethics
acts as a fence. You pass it or climb over it at your own risk. For
example, none of the leaders I work with closely are allowed to
counsel females on their own. Men have tensions with their partners. They get disillusioned. Then they find themselves emotionally
involved in counselling a girl and they embrace. There's a kiss, a
gift or wink of the eye, and he now has another option—and it
doesn't include his wife! Recently one of my leaders came to me
while we were breaking bread together and said, 'I have something
to confess.' He had broken the ethical code. He just thought he'd
help this girl. His wife was out and it wouldn't take long. She

shared her need, he briefly advised her, prayed with her and that was it. She put her arms round him and clung on tight in appreciation. He wasn't turned on. He wasn't disillusioned with his wife. He wasn't looking for gratification outside of his family. But he realised, given a different set of circumstances, where it could have led. We prayed together and he was forgiven: the code of ethics is vital if we are going to be moral.

Paul wrote to the notorious Corinthian church, 'All these things happened to them as examples—as object lessons to us—to warn us against doing the same things; they were written down so that we could read about them and learn from them in these last days as the world nears its end' (1 Cor 10:11, The Living Bible).

It is not that we don't have ethics. We ignore them. We become secretive. Secrets are rarely healthy. Archibald Hart has said, 'They destroy community, breed suspicion, and undermine trust. They function to divide loyalties and inhibit love.' Open and honest friendships have to be the key. It is unlikely that we will continually flirt with others if we are open with partners and friends. It is almost impossible to cheat the tax man if we are accountable to an accountant, advisor or board. Indeed, if anything we do has to be secretive (unless it's a surprise birthday party!) I've come to learn that it's probably ethically wrong.

Secrecy leads to independence and an unwillingness to be accountable. Without voluntary accountability we turn our own personal perspectives into the truth. Inadequate judgements are entered into, unconscious motivational factors are ignored. In a word we become deceived.

We want to be influential for God, but we cannot fuel a broad and demanding ministry on little capital of character and integrity. It is no good saying to ourselves, 'Of course, I'm an exception because of this, that or the other.' As has been said, we are not to be the *exception* but the *example*.

Openness the key

Freedom and financial sufficiency can be blessings from God. The issue is what we do with our freedom and financial blessing. We must all ask ourselves, 'Will this action or purchase help me to become the person I want to be?' When we linger over the top rack of the newsagents, or flick through channels late at night, these are the questions we need to ask. As we purchase clothes, a car, take holidays and indulge in leisure expenditure, this again and again is the question we have to ask. This is not a guilt trip, but a plea to make an honest assessment of whether our choices are helping us to become what we were called to be. Openness has to be the key. I've been married now for twenty-five years, and for too long in our marriage I have wasted a valuable natural resource—my wife's opinion! She is not always right, but she is almost always helpful. It is the unshared areas where Jesus is not Lord.

One of my favourite writers, R C Sproul, puts it like this: 'Social ethics must never be substituted for personal ethics.' Crusading can easily become a dodge for failing to face up to one's personal lack of morality. By the same token, even if I am a model of personal righteousness, that does not excuse my participation in social evil. The man who is faithful to his wife while he exercises bigotry towards his neighbour is no better than the adulterer who crusades for social justice. What God requires is justice that is both personal and social. So if we are to maintain a cutting edge we need (1) a clear message and (2) sharpness of character and morality (and a code of ethics).

Handling change

'Constant change is here to stay.' It is strange how we all tend to resist change. But if we are to maintain a personal and corporate cutting edge we must not only be open to change but expect it and plan for it. And we must help others plan for it as well. We all like to think we are flexible, full of fresh initiatives, forward thinking—but most are not. Changes are bitter-sweet.

If we are initiating changes, we are for those changes 100%. If someone else is initiating those changes we need to 'wait on the Lord'! Changes demand that we turn our backs on the comfortable structures of the past. Change is taking place around us every day: political changes, cultural changes and even changes in the law—and not in my opinion always for the better. Values have changed, leadership and personalities change; there are changes in music and even in the weather! Expectations change thus necessitating that we hold our tongues before speaking our minds.

We will never win this nation for Christ by surrounding ourselves with safe people who never change. Patterns of belief and believers left unchanged will eventually create an ineffective church. I'm not here talking about biblical truth and the eternal doctrines set out for us in Scripture. But there are many beliefs that have nothing to do with the Bible. Here we need to change.

One day a vision hit my desk in the form of a photocopied letter. It was in fact for another church, but it could have been for me and our own community. Simple and ingenious it stated, 'You've been a cruise liner but now I want you to be a battleship.' There is nothing inferior about a cruise liner. I've often wanted to go on one. A liner has a captain, deck crew, engine crew and technical teams. But cruise liners are for folk to relax in and find health, rest and get away from it all. Many dismembered, battered and bruised parts of the body of Christ have found their way onto our cruise liners. Healed and helped, are they now to grow old, fat and lethargic? No! We are being called to be a battleship. Pastoral house groups (where we were in danger of pastoring people into the ground) became action groups. Prayer and intercession groups emerged, as did social action teams, PR and media hit squads, evangelistic and literature forums, care groups for newcomers, musicians with prophetic ministries. We have in that short space of time spawned and nurtured a number of area-wide, national and international ministries.

To adjust to change I have had to deal with my own insecurity and, at times, resentment. I have felt pushed outside of the centre of things. I am often looked upon as being far too busy and sometimes far too important to be invited to this, that or the other. But we must be continually creating space for others or we die and become satisfied with limited successes. We must set others free to find God's will for their roles in life. Most will appreciate our perspectives and advice. It's nice to be wanted, but we have to understand that we can't always be wanted by all the people all the time.

D L Moody stated: 'The Bible is not given to increase our knowledge but to change our lives.' So to maintain a sharp cutting edge we must keep a clear message, develop sharp character, morality and ethics, and be willing to be an agent for change.

Upward and outward

The current outpouring of the Holy Spirit could be the least productive of many decades, unless we focus the church's attention upward and outward. There are countless books on business techniques and excellence of spirit. The church that is as organised as a sack of spanners could do well to read some of them and implement change where necessary. But if excellence is based on comparing ourselves with other ministries, churches and teams then we're finished! It is soul destroying. Jesus' best friend John, when exiled on Patmos, saw Jesus on a throne. The church of Philadelphia was never compared to the church of Smyrna. Billy Graham will not be compared to Yonggi Cho. Malcolm Muggeridge will not be compared to Alexander Solzhenitzyn. John Stott is not compared to David Watson. U2's Bono will not be compared to Cliff Richard. All churches and individuals will be compared and called to look to Jesus and his throne—his rule.

We are not to look downward and inward but upward, outward and onward. You can go to countless charismatic meetings, house groups, conferences and even celebration events and be forgiven for feeling that they live in another world. The focus is upward ('thank you, Lord') and inward ('thank you, brother/sister'). Visitors find it hard to break into this mind-set. 'Our church is so friendly,' one hears with regularity. Of course it is if you're in it! The focus of a large number of New Churches is still inward in the main. Their leadership may have an outward heart, but upward and outward must be the heart attitude of the *whole* church.

Søren Kierkegaard explains, 'We understand life backward, but we are called to look forward.' We can learn from the past and thank God for the past, but we dare not live off this capital. We must live life day by day, drawing on grace and revelation. We don't know much about the future. God has only given us a few cracks in the fence. We can see there will be no more sin or sickness, no more sadness or crying, no more devil or demons. It sounds like paradise. It is! But we need to be bringing that future into the present. The issues dividing Christians are not Calvinistic or Arminian, charismatic or non-charismatic, house church or traditional but rather how much of the kingdom should we expect now? I'm for as much as God will give us. If we seek we will find. We shall need to look upward and outward as we're brought into contact with sin and sickness. We shall need the power of the gospel to bring people through into forgiveness and deliverance. As we are touched with the sadnesses and losses of the world we shall need intercessory prayer, Scripture and the comfort of the Holy Spirit. He's good at binding up the broken-hearted. We will need love and friendship within the body of Christ—not only to model how life ought to be, but to absorb the needy into a healing environment. We shall need those relationships to act as a resource to meet the needs of others. This is not a selfish kingdom.

George Hoffman once said, 'We can't change everyone's world everywhere—but we can change someone's world somewhere.' To try to reach the needs of the world with our personal meagre resources is madness. But we can bless, influence and be agents of change somewhere for someone; in the home where we live, in the office were we work, the place where we shop, and our broader range of relationships. For those with specific ministries we can change situations in rural villages, urban and suburban districts as well as the inner cities, hospital wards, on the streets and among the elderly.

I fervently believe it is the charismatic churches, indeed all flexible evangelical churches, that have the brightest future in terms of church life. The issue we must face is this: have we the will to grasp the issues, pool our resources and work in co-operation rather than competition with each other? Have we got what it takes to become relevant, not only in our own age, but also our children's?

Once ignored, rejected and criticised we now find that charismatic church life, kingdom theology and the influences of the New Church are everywhere: in YFC, YWAM, Spring Harvest, Interdenominational magazines, Bible colleges, March for Jesus, church planting, even in the House of Lords and the House of Commons! The influences are there. We asked God to make us great, though we didn't understand that in many of our difficulties he was preparing us for greatness. Now what are we going to do with these opportunities? God deliver us from having trained so well but still missing the start of a new beginning in our race of life, fidgeting around, embarrassed, half-blind, sapped of strength and unable to run.

Upward and outward will mean different things for different people. For some it will be as ordinary as a meal with evangelicals in their locality, creating bridges of reconciliation and understanding rather than feeding misunderstanding and rumour. The Bible tells us to love our neighbours and also to love our enemies. G K Chesterton said, 'Probably because they are generally the same people!'

Church planting three miles away will be a good starting point for others. Giving up summer holidays, or time between college/ university and business to be trained in evangelism and church planting is another. Overseas trips led by apostolic teams is again a further means of investing time, money and energy into the nations of the world.

To leaders I say we must bring national and international affairs into the focus of our meetings. An hour of singing and 'thank you, Lord' prayers is often inappropriate. There is nothing wrong with an hour of worship, but when we've been doing that for fifteen years not knowing what else to do, we should have grown up by now. God grant us prayers for the nation, for the government, for the Royal Family, for the poor and marginalised expressed in our meetings. Maybe then some of those we pray for will meet with us when they see we care. At the moment, for most, they're not mentioned and if they are cared for it's not expressed in the main forum of our worship/prayer/teaching.

I called our church to pray publicly when we heard of a certain hijack. We prayed for the pilot and his crew, for the passengers and the terrorists. What a joy (and surprise!) it was to read—within hours—headlines in most of the national popular dailies: 'The Lord is with us!' The senior member of the crew was a Christian. He was praying for his passengers and sharing Christ with the terrorists. It was Oswald Chambers who wrote, 'God never gives us discernment in order that we may criticise, rather that we may intercede.'

So to keep a sharp cutting edge and to reach this nation with the gospel by the year 2000 we need to (1) maintain a clean and clear message; (2) develop godly character, morality and appropriate ethics; (3) be agents of change and train others for change; (4) look up and look out until we see the glory of God cover the earth as the water covers the sea.

Our nation for Christ by the year 2000? An impossible dream? Well, it's better to believe for the impossible than the inevitable. It doesn't mean that everybody will receive Christ's offer of forgiveness and eternal life. It does mean that all will hear, see and have the opportunity. Perhaps through television and radio, but mostly through people 'on the ground' in villages, towns and cities being good news and proclaiming good news. And when we get it wrong we shall apologise to our Lord, one another and those we are seeking to minister to.

Borrowed faith has no power. Each of us must demonstrate our commitment to the goals, objectives and the spirit of this work. We cannot have half-hearted commitment—it has to be total. If we commit ourselves to blessing those 'below' us, we won't have much opportunity to be jealous of those 'above' us in the affairs of this world. God will release his power as we move towards the year 2000 and set our eyes on that goal of reaching the nation for Christ, alongside the sending out of teams across the world.

In the year 2000 we shall be able to raise our glasses—unless the Lord has returned first—and toast 'the King and his kingdom'.

If you would like to know more about Pioneer, send a large stamped, addressed envelope to:

Pioneer
PO Box 79c
Esher
Surrey
KT10 9LP

Pioneer can supply you with their quarterly magazine and a list of teaching tapes, books and evangelistic literature which they publish through their mail order company Pioneer Direct.